Great Reset and The New Deal After Covid-19

Fatma Özkul, Sonat Bayram (eds.)

Great Reset and The New Deal After Covid-19

PETER LANG

Bibliographic Information published by the Deutsche Nationalbibliothek
The Deutsche Nationalbibliothek lists this publication in the Deutsche Nationalbibliografie; detailed bibliographic data is available online at http://dnb.d-nb.de.

Library of Congress Cataloging-in-Publication Data
A CIP catalog record for this book has been applied for at the Library of Congress.

ISBN 978-3-631-86795-2 (Print)
E-ISBN 978-3-631-86796-9 (E-PDF)
E-ISBN 978-3-631-89350-0 (E-PUB)
10.3726/b20387

Peter Lang – Berlin · Bruxelles · Lausanne · New York · Oxford

This publication has been peer reviewed.

www.peterlang.com

Table of Contents

List of Contributors

Sonat Bayram
Asst. Prof. Dr, Trakya Üniversitesi, Faculty of Applied Sciences, Banking and Finance Department

İ. Burçak Vatansever Durmaz
Asst. Prof. Dr., Bahçeşehir University, Vocational School of Health

Sinem Eray
Dr., Bahçeşehir University, Graduate School

Zülfiye Gül Ercan
Assoc. Prof. Trakya University Education Faculty, Preschool Education Department, zgulercan@trakya.edu.tr
ORCID ID: 0000-0002-7532-5251

Feyza Nazan Gündüz
Dr. Trakya University, Foreign Affairs Department, feyzanazangunduz@trakya.edu.tr
ORCID ID: 0000-0001-9505-8560

İsmail Orçun Gündüz
Prof. Dr, Trakya Üniversitesi, Faculty of Applied Sciences, Banking and Finance Department

İ. Sadi Uzunoğlu
Prof. Dr, Trakya Üniversitesi, Faculty of Applied Sciences, Banking and Finance Department

İpek Senem Gedikoğlu
PhD Student, Bahçeşehir Universtiy

Gökhan Sönmezler
Prof. Dr, Trakya Üniversitesi, Faculty of Applied Sciences, Banking and Finance Department

Editor Note

The World Economic Forum prepared a manifesto-like statement and opened the issue of the great reset to discussion. The Great Reset lays out the main idea of rebuilding the world economy and redesigning capitalism in the wake of the Covid-19 pandemic. The idea is emerging that the biggest crisis after the Great Depression in 1929 is currently being experienced due to Covid-19 and that Covid-19 will have very serious and long-term effects on economic growth, public debt, employment, and human welfare. The idea of the Great Reset is explained under seven main headings: capitalizing on the fourth industrial revolution, strengthening regional development, stimulating global cooperation, developing sustainable business models, improving the health of the environment, redesigning social contracts, skills, and jobs, and shaping economic recovery.

According to the fathers of the Great Reset, for the world to recover after Covid-19, radical changes should be made in many areas from education to social contracts and working conditions, countries should act together, and all industries should be transformed in accordance with new conditions and ways of working. Because the Covid-19 pandemic will have serious and long-term consequences on economic growth, public debt, employment and human welfare, and these results will increase social tension, combined with the already worsening global warming and environmental problems, the tangle of problems will grow. When increasing income inequality is added to all these, a very fragile economic structure will be encountered and policies to save the day will be insufficient. Therefore, economic, and social systems need to be built from scratch on new foundations.

The digital transformation, which started with the fourth industrial revolution and accelerated during the Covid-19 process, will cause the growth of technology companies the most. The rapid digital transformation seen in education, health, sports, banking, and e-commerce will increase the importance of the cyber security sector. The companies that grew very fast during the epidemic have been the companies that have adapted to the new trends and provided the best customer service in both in-store and online sales. In this regard, the main idea in micro reset is there is a future after Covid-19 for companies that can adapt to new trends and make the necessary transformation, but those who cannot adapt will not survive in the post-covid world.

Discussions on the production and consumption of information in the world are increasingly moving forward. Information technologies used in the production of knowledge are also developing and diversifying day by day. Information technologies have an important role in the formation of today's living conditions. The increasing prevalence of these technologies helps to improve many jobs and life processes. The Covid-19 pandemic process, which appears as a period when habits must change, forces individuals to be more careful in all areas. In this process, where we must realize old habits in different ways, the new possibilities offered by information technologies allow us to digitize all processes faster than ever before. By using mobile phones, computers, and tablets without being in physical contact, all information processes can continue without slowing down. According to some opinions, it is thought that the digitalization process has accelerated with the pandemic. When information technologies are mentioned, technologies consisting of hardware, software and networks come to mind. These technologies can be physical as well as non-physical possibilities.

Fatma Özkul, Sonat Bayram
İSTANBUL, SEPTEMBER / 2022

Sonat Bayram

Preface Great Reset and the New Era with Different Perspectives

Covid 19 – The pandemic period has caused a new transformation in every field. Starting from people's consumer habits, with the change to human resources, working behaviors and durations in workplaces have been affected and digitalization has created a new space. A more unified and digital world has also had an impact on the governments of states. The fact that everyone can easily access every information and product they want over the internet has affected the interaction between countries due to trade. In this process, countries had to go through changes to keep up with the world. However, the biggest impact of the pandemic has been in the education system. The closure of schools and the online education process continued from home has changed the way of education all over the world. The area where digital transformation was felt the most was the finance and banking sector. Digitization, which is the result of working from home, has now enabled people to perform transactions without the need to physically go to the bank. All the areas mentioned here constitute the main chapters of the book and are explained in detail below.

Covid 19 and Consumption Expenditures: The Covid-19 pandemic process, which has caused changes in many areas in a short time around the world, has also affected consumption practices and consumer behaviors. Many factors such as curfews applied to reduce the effects of the epidemic, mandatory quarantine periods, stopping of entry and exit between countries, intercity travel restrictions, and the uneasiness of virus contamination due to the inability to maintain social distance in crowded environments have brought about significant changes in consumer behavior. Numerous new researches on changing consumer behavior have been made and published (Erkan, 2020:). With the increasing effect of the pandemic, the shopping activities of consumers have started to change (Güven, 2020).

Changing consumer behavior related to the process has brought along many new and special research. DORinsight, a market research company with the largest authorized database in Turkey with over 1 million registered members, conducted a study on "Changing consumer behavior after the epidemic" with the participation of 5,007 people over the age of 18 between 15 and 20 April 2020. Results on how purchasing behaviors are affected have been obtained.

According to the results of the research, 92 % of the female participants and 84 % of the male participants stated that their purchasing behavior has changed, and 60 % of them stated that their monthly expenditures have increased in this process. According to purchasing preferences, the food sector ranked first with 69 %, while hygiene products ranked second with 60 %. In meeting the needs, 60 % of the participants gave importance to hygiene, 15 % to price, 12 % to accessibility, 92 % to quality, and 4 % to speed. According to the results of the research, 86 % of the participants stated that the use of social media increased during the Covid-19 pandemic (DORinsight, 2020).

Even though consumer behavior has shown some differences according to regions or cultures, it can be said that it basically changes in the same direction with different accelerations. According to the research results of the Nielsen Research company, two weeks after the first officially determined case statement of the USA on January 30, 2020, the sales of medical products such as disinfectants and masks, respectively, compared to the previous week; An increase of 4 %, 47 % and 53 % was observed. In Turkey, on the night of March 10, 2020, when the first case was announced, and on the following day, there was a simultaneous increase in demand for proactive and reactive health products and kitchen products related to "pantry preparation". This shows that in the global world, the processes of crises differ according to countries (NielsenIQ, 2020).

With the widespread use of the internet, which is used in all parts of society today, people's behaviors, habits and shopping styles have changed significantly as well as their lives. (Turan, 2008). Rapid changes in the information age have brought about rapid developments in the use of technology. This development, which affects all areas of life, has also affected the way and understanding of trade of consumers (Akçi & Annaç Göv, 2015). As a result of the increase in e-commerce volumes, the development of mobile applications for online shopping, and the increase in payment and delivery options, there is a serious growth in e-commerce all over the world day by day.

Although the retail sector has weakened due to reasons such as people staying at home because of the Covid-19 pandemic and curfews around the world and the anxiety of disease transmission, electronic commerce has begun to experience its golden age (Güven, 2020). The changing consumer behaviors and lifestyles with the epidemic have radically affected the digital transformation process and brought it to a completely different point.

The use of television and the internet has increased, and visitor traffic has increased significantly in e-commerce (Yıldız, 2020). In this period, e-commerce sites selling on the internet also turned the process into an advantage. As the market share of e-commerce companies has increased, many of them have either revised their existing e-commerce platform or started to establish a new e-commerce platform.

Human Resources and Digital Transformation: The globalization and industrialization process experienced throughout the world has changed the way businesses operate, business relations, long-term returns of the business, professions, and the perspective of manpower (Türkel & Yeşilkuş, 2020). Due to the intense competitive environment, almost all organizations are now focusing on providing access to Human Resources services through technology and web-based applications.

Digital transformation: It is possible to say that it is a worldwide topic of great importance for businesses in all sectors, as it changes customer relations, internal processes, and value creation. In this transformation, the main concern of the stakeholders is to define a vision and roadmap that determines the way forward (Zaoui & Souissi, 2020) Human Resources Management, updated in the light of digital developments, now appears as a new generation "digital" Human Resources (Doğan, 2011).

Human Resources Management systems realized with the advantages of digital transformation; It enables companies to obtain, record, update and easily access data related to the knowledge, skills and abilities of employees in companies. This can be a factor that helps Human Resources professionals to make faster and more effective decisions for businesses. With the help of computers, data obtained in digital format faster and more accurately can be analyzed in different ways, and the results of these can be transmitted to business managers in different formats (Calp & Doğan, 2019).

Innovative supported Human Resources Management applications help businesses to create a more effective and strategically targeted human capital. Information technologies allow data to be interpreted quickly and accurately, thus allowing qualitative and quantitative data for Human Resources to progress in parallel with business strategies (Lazazzara & Galanaki, 2018).

It is in question that digital transformation will change the labor market according to the labor force needed in any business field. Human Resources professionals need to embrace this change and move forward by adapting to this change. At this point, for future professions and occupational groups to find a certain place in the business world under the effects of digital transformation and to show continuity, the qualities and direction of the career services that the HR Unit will provide to employees to discover and develop the skills they need are critical (Karacan, Özdemir & Ayaz, 2020).

New Capitalism: Crises have a very important place in capitalism. In an environment where the effects of the 2008 crisis, caused by the lack of control and instability in the global financial system, have not completely disappeared, capitalism faced a new crisis at the end of 2019.

The Covid-19 crisis has not only led to results that will shape the period we are in, but also has created dynamics that will change and transform economic, political, cultural, and technological developments in the global system. Although the Covid-19 crisis is a development in the field of health, it has a structural depth that cannot be handled only in this context. In capitalism, which operates according to the logic of "maximizing everything", the effect of the mode of production on working conditions is most evident in the field of health. In addition, the fact that production takes place at the expense of the destruction of nature triggers crises in the field of health. Globalization makes it very easy for such crises to spread all over the world in a short time. The Covid-19 crisis has intensified the discussions on how to shape a new order for the functioning of the global system, as well as the devastating picture caused by capitalism and globalization intertwined with it.

The Covid-19 crisis has caused capitalism to re-face the systemic problems that emerged after the 2008 global financial crisis. In many of the Global North, inequality and wealth concentration have increased significantly as low-income workforces have increased, social protection spending has decreased, and austerity policies have been implemented. In 2019, 43.4 % of global net wealth was in the hands of 1 %. Inequality in the Global South continued to rise rapidly.

Wage increases in the global north also remained below growth, thus increasing inequality in income distribution and welfare. The skewness in the income distribution in favor of the richest segment decreased aggregate demand and suppressed the demand for consumer goods. This has led manufacturers in the northern regions to shift their production to the south, where labor is cheaper (Lawrence, 2020).

Since capitalism is a profit-oriented system, technological progress is the most important tool of every firm in the capitalist system. Thanks to the technological progress, although the companies can increase their profits by producing at a lower cost than their competitors, over time it causes other companies to follow a similar strategy, and as a result, the profit rates decrease with the increase in the organic composition of the capital. Decreasing rates of profit is the most critical element of capitalism. According to Marx, who sees the periodic crises of capitalism as the most obvious expression of capitalism's internal contradictions, crises are mechanisms that play a regulatory role against the fluctuations that occur in capitalism. The mode of production peculiar to capitalism is organized by the expansion of capital on class relations based on exploitation (Giddens, 2018).

The Covid-19 outbreak should not be considered only as a crisis in the field of health. The dynamics of change brought about by every crisis are also valid for Covid-19. It is not just that the roles of the state have changed; The future of globalization, possible developments in the supra-national structure like the EU, the path to be followed by democracies and the struggles that will arise in leading the global system are the most curious subjects in the new world order after Covid19. Although there is broad agreement that economic factors such as capital, technology, and production move in the same direction as liberalization since the end of the Cold War, current and global problems such as Covid-19 raise serious doubts about the sustainability of this framework. (McNamara & Newman, 2020).

Another important issue highlighted by the Covid-19 crisis is the re-discovery of the state as a very important actor in the economy and in ensuring global coordination. Especially in developed countries where the health system is in the hands of the private sector, the collapse of the system and its inability to respond to the needs of its citizens have caused very serious consequences. The state has stepped in in many areas such as the expropriation of failing companies, the operation of credit mechanisms through public resources.

In the new process, the state will come to the fore more in economy and other fields. It is possible to state that this new position of the state will come to the fore not only as the authority that carries out public expenditures, but also as an element that is compatible with digitalization and that needs to increase its institutional capacity to ensure that this digitalization operates efficiently in the economy, education, health and other fields. In other words, the Covid-19 crisis will also transform states. The devastating picture caused when the most basic needs of the society such as education and health are left to the leadership of the private sector, compels this transformation.

Effects of Covid 19 on Gender Inequality: While gender-based inequalities at the global level were an important agenda item before the pandemic, these inequalities deepen in the conditions brought about by the pandemic. Gender-based inequalities, violence and abuse have increased throughout the world during the pandemic process. The Covid-19 pandemic has affected daily life in many ways. One of them is the economic and social effects on women. As always in times of crisis, women's disadvantaged positions in the labor market worsen, unpaid care work increases, and gender-based violence and abuse become widespread. In addition, the intervention methods for these violations are also affected by the crisis and are often ineffective.

As a result of the interruption of face-to-face education due to the pandemic, the need for home care of children has increased. In addition, the increasing needs of family elders are added to this. It is thought that women, who are accepted as the "natural addressees" of the increasing care need in this way, have problems in continuing to work and that women will be affected more than men in possible dismissals. This situation reinforces the disadvantaged position of women in employment and causes an increase in vulnerabilities.

Considering that women have limited access to policies such as paid leave or social protection at the time of dismissal, this becomes even more important in cases where the income of the household is covered only by women.

There are differences between mothers and fathers in terms of job loss rates. In the study conducted by Andrew et al., which compared wage-earning mothers and fathers, the rate of temporarily losing their job was 34 % for mothers, 30 % for fathers; permanently, it is 16 % and 11 %, respectively (Andrew et al., 2020). Therefore, regardless of whether it is permanent or temporary, the rate of quitting or dismissal of mothers is higher than that of fathers.

In addition to business life, women feel the unbalanced division of labor, which already exists in their home life, more intensely during the pandemic process. In other words, the inequality between men and women in domestic life, which existed before the pandemic, has increased with the pandemic. According to research, women around the world work 2.5 times more for home care than men; However, they do not receive the rewards of their labor compared to men (United Nations Development Program, 2020a).

Past studies have shown that prior to the COVID-19 pandemic, women received support from another family member or domestic worker, despite the unequal division of responsibilities within the home. However, with the restrictions applied and other measures taken to prevent the spread of the virus during the pandemic process, this support of women has been difficult or has completely disappeared. At the same time, with the increase in the time spent at home, women's responsibilities towards the home have also increased. Household members who could not get support from outside in this process had to fulfil their responsibilities themselves.

In addition to the increase in the responsibilities of women working in domestic care, the intensity and frequency of the work done by women who did not work before the pandemic and fulfilled their responsibilities for housework increased with the pandemic. One of the main reasons for this increase is the increase in the length of stay of individuals in the household during the pandemic process. As the number of people spending time at home increases, the number and intensity of work to be done at home also increases. Therefore, women must struggle with more strenuous physical conditions. On the other hand, it is thought that unemployed women have more psychological difficulties in this process, and this difficulty is also associated with their financial situation. Unemployed women make a living with the income of other individuals when there is no financial source of income. These people can be family elders, siblings as well as spouses. For example, 1.5 million women in Turkey live financially dependent on their spouses, and when the groups affected during the pandemic are compared, it is known that poor women living in dependence on their spouses are the most vulnerable group in the society (Bayar, Günçavdı & Levent, 2020).

Digital Transformation in Education After Covid-19: The Covid-19 pandemic has affected education systems around the world, causing the temporary closure of education and training institutions at all levels, from pre-school to higher education. According to UNESCO data, as of April 29, 2020, approximately 1,725,082,528 students were affected due to the closure of schools due to the epidemic, and physical education was interrupted in 186 countries nationwide and in many countries on a local basis, affecting more than 90 % of the world's student population (UNESCO, 2020a).

The concept of distance education, online learning or e-learning is used as a general name for content dissemination and rapid learning methods through the application of information technology and internet technology (Zhou et al., 2020). The Distance Education Model was considered as a suitable solution model by experts and administrators, especially in all countries where epidemic cases were experienced intensively, and was implemented quickly (Yamamoto & Altun, 2020).

The most important factor accelerating the transition to distance education is technology. Technology development in the education sector has affected the execution of educational activities, accelerated the formation of new models, and strengthened the interaction of academics and students with digital applications (Şener ve Gündüzalp, 2018). There are many 19 digital applications in education, such as the use of open education methods, synchronous and asynchronous lectures, sharing of course materials in the virtual environment (Harley, 2002). In addition, many innovations such as distance education programs, digital certificate programs, the execution of lecture notes and homework over the system, and the realization of student and academician activities on academic and student information systems lead higher education to digital transformation within the framework of the trends brought by Industry 4.0 (Şener ve Gündüzalp, 2018).

In pre-school education, some private school nurseries have also switched to distance education. However, for parents, the screen time applications of children at this age contradict the idea of distance education. For primary school students, it is observed that there are problems with concentration in distance education, and the workload of parents is high because they are young.

Effects of Covid 19 on Finance and Banking Sector and Financial Technologies: It can be said that the banking sector is one of the sectors most affected by the rapidly digitalizing climate of the world. The concentration and widespread use of the internet and smart phones with each passing day has led to the diversification of customers' demands and expectations, and ultimately to the development of technologies used in the banking sector. One of the advantages of digital transformation in the banking sector is that it reduces costs and increases efficiency, as well as perfecting the customer experience (Akın, 2020).

Today, it is noteworthy that the differences between the economies of developed and developing countries are essentially technology-based. It seems possible to complete economic growth thanks to the competencies gained by realizing effective and efficient technological investments in every sector.

Banking is one of the sectors most affected by the epidemic. According to the report prepared by the international consultancy firm PWC in the first wave of the epidemic, it was determined that the epidemic affected the banking sector under four important headings on operational, credit risk, funding cost and change in customer behavior. In this context, banks prepared crisis management action plans and ensured uninterrupted services through regular communication with their internal and external stakeholders. The continuation of the crisis revealed the credit risk of the businesses whose activities slowed down and the failure of individual customers who lost their income to fulfil their credit obligations. The environment of trust, which was lost with the epidemic, increased the funding cost of banks, and caused a cost change. More importantly, Covid-19 has led to changes in customer needs and behaviors. The change in spending preferences has increased the active use of alternative distribution channels (PWC, 2020).

According to the Covid-19 report prepared by Deloitte, an international consultancy company, in April 2020, it was concluded that public banks acted more actively and performed better than private banks in the first wave of the epidemic. It was concluded that public banks were more successful than private banks in meeting the demands of more individual and SME customers, especially in April. In addition, Public Banks, Religious Contents, Local Marketplaces, National Market Chains, Internet TV, Private Health and Media are listed as the winning sectors of the Covid-19 period among the sectors whose digital interaction is examined comparatively under 60 categories, while Private Banks, Foreign Marketplaces, Discount Markets, Culture, Cinema, Public-Health, Social Media sectors were listed as the losers of the period. (Deloitte, 2020).

Digital transformation in the banking sector with the advancements in mobile technology that shows itself first, then with internet banking, mobile banking continued as, nowadays, artificial intelligence, Internet of things, big data, and open banking, such as that eliminates the boundaries of technology, as well as the delivery of banking services blockchain technology shapes also vary with the developments that are more used to it. The technologies used with digital transformation in the banking sector and their effects on the banking sector are discussed in the titles Blockchain, Artificial Intelligence, API, Big Data, and Internet of Things.

Today, with the widespread use of the internet and the developments in digital devices such as computers and mobile phones, the banking sector is one of the sectors where the digital transformation process is experienced with the highest intensity. It can be stated that factors such as reducing costs and increasing revenues in the competitive climate of banks as well as changing

preferences, habits and expectations of bank customers are among the parameters that lead banks to digital transformation. The digitalization process in the banking sector; In the banking sector between 1998 and 2002, digital banking 1.0, 2003–2008 period digital banking 2.0, 2009–2014 period digital banking 3.0, and digital banking 4.0 in the period from 2015 to the present, are discussed and examined in four stages (Akın, 2019)

The integration of financial technology companies and start-ups that emerged with the digital transformation into banking is gaining importance. In this process of changing competitive conditions, accelerating technology and new applications that enter our lives push the sector's business model structure and consumer service channels to constantly change and develop. FinTech collaborations, which are an important part of banks' technology investments and strategies, are important for innovation investments, the future of the sector and its competitiveness.

With the increase in mobilization, people's payment habits have begun to change. The use of credit cards or cash has now been replaced by mobile applications, and payment systems have been moved to new platforms created using the infrastructure of banks, with integrations from all sectors. Companies operating in different sectors have made large investments in terms of differentiation in service with payment software integrated with banks from both their websites and mobile applications. The digitalization step that emerged with the "Banking as a Service" approach is called a model in which licensed banks integrate digital banking services directly into the products of other non-bank businesses (Gera, 2017).

As the financial sector is struggling with the real and potential repercussions of the pandemic, more "breathing space" (BIS 2020) is likely to be given, which is predicted to cause the wave of financial regulation brought about by the Global Financial Crisis. While some tax havens will be seized to slow or even reverse the crisis, most governments are expected to support a faster transition to a cashless society. Second, the challenges faced by smaller businesses and the economies of scale brought about by new technologies may result in continued divergence in the Food and Beverage Services value chains and greater firm-level consolidation within Food & Beverage Services. Third, the FinTech industry, which has enjoyed a decade of investment boom, is now facing a hurdle. While there is a growing need for new digital financial technology, many FinTech start-ups have become more difficult to fund during the recession, which will give traditional banks and especially big tech companies an edge. Fourth, businesses will need to turn to lawyers and consultants to handle the crisis and beyond. This is because they strive to find cost-effective solutions. Planning and oversight of their finances by accountants and auditors will become more important as the crisis undermines their financial stability. As a result, although employment in the financial services sector, especially in banking, is stagnant or declining, the upward trend in commercial services is expected to continue after the pandemic. (Wójcik, D. & Ioannou, S., 2020).

As more tech firms acquire licenses for digital banking, banks will not be able to operate as they used to. Nor will they be able to claim to have provided the necessary "lifelines" for their customers if they do not show that they take immediate action in emergencies such as the Covid 19 pandemic period. If they hope to acquire customers, as major digital companies do, incumbent banks must adapt and see themselves as part of the ecosystems they support (Arner vd., 2020). For this reason, it can be said that the steps to be taken in the field of digital banking operate under the obligation of improving the digitalization capabilities of the banks to a degree that will give their customers sufficient confidence in terms of both retaining the customer base and reducing the future technological uncertainty for bank customers.

The Covid-19 outbreak is expected to change the dynamics and to meet the trend of tightening bank requirements. Firms need significant liquidity support because of the large-scale shutdown and stagnation of economic activity. To do this, central banks have implemented a series of policies aimed at providing liquidity to banks and lending to the economy. The amended TLTRO-III (Targeted Longer-Term Refinancing Operations) and reintroduced LTRO (Long Term Refinancing Operations) policies are two examples of the ECB's (European Central Bank) simplified collateral compliance standards.

Regulators and supervisors have also relaxed several laws to avoid the credit crunch and reduce the circularity of policies implemented over the previous two decades. Supervisors have specifically provided temporary and operational relief to banks by enabling banks to make full use of their capital and liquidity buffers, adding additional latitude to credit classification standards, and introducing IFSR 9. Basel IV and 2020 have implemented stress tests, and several judgments have also been postponed in the jurisdiction. (Carletti vd., 2020).

It can be said that banks are at significant risk of lending to sectors susceptible to COVID-19 and serve as a warning to other emerging and developing countries that often experience poor asset quality, high NPL ratios and looser regulatory and policy frameworks. It is predictable that COVID-19 will likely cause banks to experience capital and financial difficulties in all economies. However, the results should be evaluated in the light of several limitations. First of all, relatively simple stress test models are used in the evaluation; secondly, an evaluation can be made at public banks (due to data constraints); and third, the stress test model used does not account for tax adjustments (Barua, B., & Barua, S., 2021).

In addition, studies have shown that the negative impact of the COVID-19 shock on banks is much more pronounced and long-lasting than companies and other non-bank financial institutions and revealed the expectation that banks will absorb at least some of them. The shock in the corporate sectors also saw larger banks and public banks experience further declines in stock returns, reflecting their greater role in coping with the crisis. Banks with less pre-crisis liquidity also experienced greater declines in yields, consistent with their greater vulnerability to such a shock.

In addition, studies have implied that the negative effects of the COVID-19 shock on banks are much more severe and widespread compared to companies and other non-bank financial institutions and show the expectation that banks will at least partially absorb the shock to the corporate sector. Also, larger banks and public banks experienced greater declines in stock returns, reflecting their greater role in overcoming the crisis. As would be expected given their increased sensitivity to such a shock, banks with lower pre-crisis liquidity also saw higher decreases in their returns.

More than 400 policy announcements made between February and April 2020 were analyzed to assess the effects of liquidity support, prudential measures, borrower relief and monetary policy measures on bank abnormal returns. The resulting findings suggest that actions to promote liquidity and assist borrowers have the greatest beneficial effects on banks' abnormal returns. Announcing debt relief measures increased abnormal returns while providing the greatest benefits to banks with less liquidity.

In developing countries with less room for fiscal expansion, similar policies have not been found to have a positive effect on bank stock values because they are based on government spending. Prudent management has been found to have a negative impact on bank returns, suggesting that markets are pricing in the risk of declining capital buffers. The fact that policy rate cuts primarily benefit banks with less liquidity confirms that monetary policy once again played an important role in this crisis.

Overall, the findings highlight that the crisis, and the countercyclical lending role they must play, has placed banking systems around the world with varying effects depending on the characteristics and pre-crisis vulnerabilities of each system. While certain policy interventions such as liquidity support, borrower assistance and quantitative easing may reduce this negative impact for some banks, this is not always the case for all institutions or in all cases. For example, debtor relief programs have increased the pressure on banks located in countries with limited budget space. These vulnerabilities will need to be watched closely as the pandemic continues to wreak havoc on the world's economies (Demirgüç-Kunt, A., Pedraza, A., & Ruiz-Ortega, C., 2021).

When the economic crisis caused by the Covid-19 pandemic is examined, the relationship between bank profit and risk and the use of non-interest income sources, the economic impact of the pandemic has led to stricter credit criteria and a decline in demand for many different types of loans. It has been observed that non-interest income of banks during the pandemic period is inversely proportional to risk, but positively related to performance. In the period when Covid-19 spread rapidly and affected the economy, the diversification effect brought about using non-interest income streams and the performance effect seem to be compatible. Considering the development in financial innovation in the last 20–30 years, it has been seen that the adoption of fintech has increased the financial performance of banks and also positively affected profitability, and it has been the savior of the banks, which showed the necessary importance to innovation especially during the Covid period (Li, X., Feng, H., Zhao, S., & Carter, D.A., 2021).

Gökhan Sönmezler, İsmail Orçun Gündüz, and İ. Sadi Uzunoğlu

Chapter 1 Change in Consumption Expenditures in Turkey during the Pandemic Process

Introduction

Creative destruction is a macroeconomic term that describes the process. The concept introduced by Joseph Schumpeter can be defined as "constantly revolutionizing the economic structure from within, constantly destroying the old one, constantly creating a new one". In this respect, Schumpeter used creative destruction to describe the power that allows new actors to quickly enter an existing market and establish themselves alongside or instead of existing companies (Loeschevc and Torre, 2020). In this respect, the most important factor that creates creative destruction is the behavior of consumers. Because individuals react to this in extraordinary events and tend to different points in consumer behavior. Behavioral changes of consumers, on the other hand, ensure the survival of companies that adapt to it; It brings about the disappearance of companies that cannot keep up. In other words, the society has the power to bring production from one market segment and from one location to another with the demand it creates. Therefore, in this study, we will try to show the new "situations" that this will create for companies by examining the consumer behavior of consumers during the Covid 19 pandemic period. In the first part of the study, consumers' reactions to Covid 19 will be discussed within the framework of the RCA model and Maslow's needs pyramid, in order to see how consumers, react in periods such as Covid 19. Afterwards, the differences and similarities between these reactions and consumer behavior in Turkey will be analyzed. At this stage, the reaction of consumers in Turkey during the Covid 19 pandemic will be examined through card spending.

Consumer Behavior and Maslow's Needs Pyramid

One of the first studies on understanding consumer behavior is Maslow's "Hierarchy of Needs" study. Abraham Maslow, in his work in 1943, created a five-step pyramid as seen below.

When we order the pyramid of needs from the top to the bottom, the following order emerges:

- Need for self-actualization (virtue, creativity, spontaneity, problem solving, non-judgment, acceptance of facts)
- The need for esteem (self-respect, confidence, achievement, respect of others, respect for others)
- The need for belonging, love, affection (friendship, family, sexual intimacy)
- Safety need (body, job, resource, ethics, family, health, property security)

Physiological needs (breath, food, water, sexuality, sleep, balance, excretion) Maslow, while expressing human behaviors in a hierarchy that divides human behaviors into five levels in the pyramid of needs, also divides these levels into two groups: deficiency needs and growth needs. Deficiency needs consist of the first four levels in the pyramid and are the basic needs of people. The first two groups of expenditures that meet the deficiency needs are a reflection of the psychology of survival, which expresses the need for self-protection of people (Yuen et al., 2021). In this respect, expenditures for deficiency needs prevent expenditures related to growth needs, as they provide individuals with a greater sense of control in their lives. In this respect, there is a tendency to meet the basic needs of people without turning to their optional growth needs ((Yuen et al., 2021). A deficiency or problem experienced at any level in the hierarchy of Maslow's pyramid prevents the person from moving to the next level. For example, for a person who cannot meet his physical needs such as nutrition and sleep, it will not be possible to talk about the need for security, which constitutes the second stage in the pyramid, such as the ownership of a house that will keep him safe (Şeker, 2014).

When we bring together the consumption expenditure categories and Maslow's pyramid of needs, the figure above emerges. In this connection, spending patterns differ with income. While expenditures in the low-income group are mostly directed towards basic needs expenditures, the picture can be completely different as income increases. In this respect, the proportional weight of useful expenditures and discretionary expenditures increases with increasing income.

Consumer Behavior during the Pandemic Period

Covid-19, which first appeared in Wuhan, China in December 2019, then spread rapidly to the rest of the globe. As a result of this development, the World Health Organization declared the disease a pandemic on March 11, 2020. After this

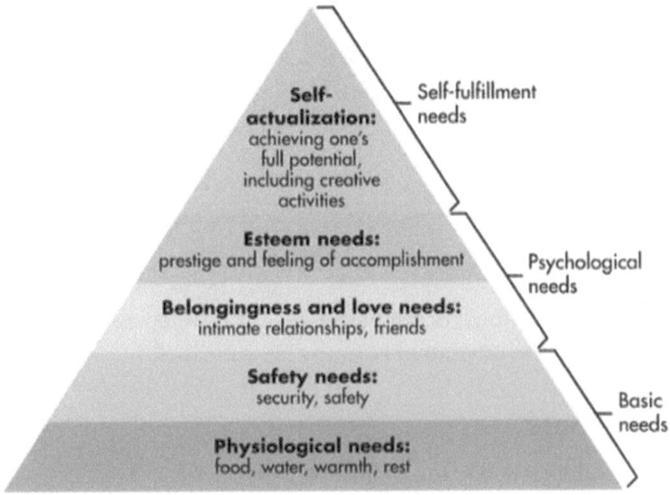

Figure 1.1: Maslow's Needs Pyramid

date, the disease still poses a serious health threat with many variant forms. Many people are affected by the disease, or because of the psychological state that occurs even if the disease is not infected. In short, Covid 19 has had an impact on the lives of all people, whether infected or not.

The effect of Covid 19 on people's lives naturally causes people to react to this situation. To explain this process, Kirk and Rifkin and Guthrie et al. Researches such as these use the RCA model. According to this model, when societies encounter a crisis, they first react to the new situation, then they accept the difficulties and try to cope with them, and the situation reached in the last stage is fully accepted and creates a new normal in social life. The RCA model has a structure that shows how consumer behavior develops in a temporal dimension in the Covid 19 pandemic. In this respect, in this study, we will consider the effect of the Covid 19 pandemic on consumer behavior within the framework of the RCA model stages (Kirk & Rifkin, 2020; Guthrie et al., 2021).

The RCA model is a simple model that describes how consumer behavior evolves over time. There are three stages in this model, which can be briefly expressed in the figure above. In the first stage, according to the model, when consumers encounter a major event or crisis in their lives, they give a first reaction to this event. In the second stage, accepting new events and coping with them comes with it. In the third and final stage, it is the stage of adapting to the

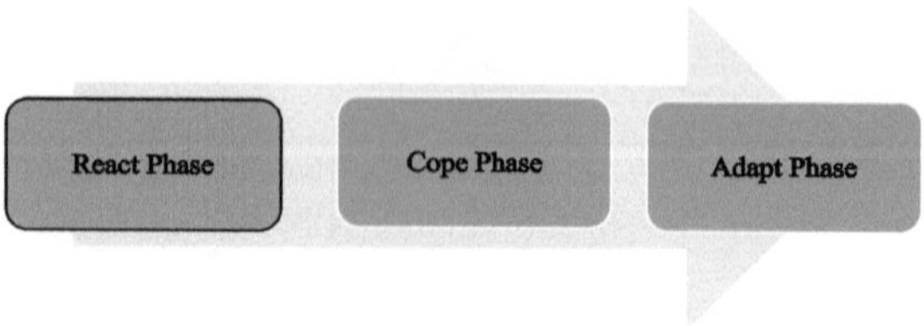

Figure 1.2: Model RCA

situation that occurs within the framework of the developments experienced by the consumers with the crisis, that is, to the 'new normal'.

Responsive Phase

People have developed a reaction against this effect in their behavior with Covid-19. People have different ways of living and working. Besides, what they buy and how they buy is different (Accenture, 2020). In this regard, the reactions to the Covid-19 pandemic may differ within the framework of people's lifestyles, thoughts and expectations. We can see that the Covid 19 pandemic has basically two effects on consumers. First, if we look at the economic-based effects, the fear of consumers losing their jobs and decreasing their incomes has increased the need for financial security and the unnecessary expenditures have been reduced (Eger et al., 2021), (Accenture, 2020). It is possible to see the effect of consumers' concerns about income and economy in Table 1.1.

While the world economy contracted by 3.1 % in 2020, when the pandemic period was intense, the size of this contraction reached 4.5 % in developed countries. In the same period, while world trade decreased by 8.2 %, there were dramatic decreases in exports and imports. While this situation increases the fears of consumers about losing their jobs and decreasing income, this fear shows differences according to factors such as gender and age. For example, although there is no gender difference in the effects of the pandemic on job loss, women are more concerned about a decrease in their income than men and tend to reduce their current consumption (Dang & Nguyen, 2021). On the other hand, while millennials are more afraid of job and income loss, boomers are generally less afraid of retirees.

The level of fear and fear towards the crisis is important in terms of understanding the process. Because as the fear of the crisis grows, people's reactions tend to grow. The area where the pandemic creates fear on consumers is about

Table 1.1: Economic growth in some selected regions (%)

	2019	2020	2021 (Expectation)
Earth	2.8	–3.1	5.9
Developed countries	1.7	–4.5	5.2
USA	2.2	–3.4	6.0
EU	1.3	–6.3	5.0
Developing countries	3.7	–2.1	6.4
World Trade Volume	0.9	–8.2	9.7
Imports			
Developed countries	2.0	–9.0	9.0
Developing countries	–0.6	–8.0	12.1
Export			
Developed countries	1.2	–9.4	8.0
Developing countries	0.4	–5.2	11.6

Source: IMF, World Economic Outlook, October 2021.

health. The first effect of this fear on consumer behavior was panic buying. Panic buying behavior of storable consumer goods in times of natural disasters or man-made crises is a common phenomenon (Keane and Neal, 2021, p. 102). During the Covid 19 pandemic, the panic buying behavior of consumers was primarily aimed at basic food needs for the basic layer of Maslow's hierarchy of needs. Later, for the safety needs, which is the second layer of the Maslow hierarchy, a trend towards protective sanitary items such as mask disinfectants has occurred (Eger et al., 2021, p. 9), (Loxton et al., 2020, pp. 11–12). As the number of coronavirus cases increases, stockpiling of food, medicine and other supplies has increased all over the world (Auitin, 2020).

A change in consumer behavior is often accompanied by environmental stimuli. Natural disasters and health crises are such large and rapid environmental changes that they can cause changes in consumer behavior. Such extreme and rapid changes can suppress an individual's cognitive ability to handle the situation and cause more intensely emotional responses. This reaction may cause individuals to purchase excessive amounts of goods when they expect shortages or price increases in a crisis (Yuen et al., 2021). Survival psychology, which occurs with a loss of control because of not being able to cope with the crisis, also explains the panic buying behavior in a crisis (Gupta et al., 2021). In survival psychology, which tends to the first four levels in Maslow's hierarchy, the primitive part of the brain tends to be more dominant and encourages individuals to focus on the most vital needs for survival (Yuen et al., 2021). Already in this period, the common point among all over-bought products is that they can protect consumers against the virus or there is a perception in this direction (Loxton et al.,2020). Naturally, stockpiling out of fear of scarcity or the desire to survive is a rational behavior. But as a result, it is inevitable that it will cause panic and supply shortages (Islam et al., 2021, p. 10). In addition, excessive demand for certain goods with panic buying may cause insufficient supply and lead to inflation with opportunistic behaviors (Loxton et al.,2020).

Social distancing is one of the factors that significantly affect consumer behavior with the pandemic period. The slowing of the spread of the virus by practices such as wearing masks and social distancing has made practices that distance people from each other widespread. In this framework, practices such as staying at home or sheltering in place have brought social distancing (Kirk & Rifkin, 2020). The threat posed by the virus and the resulting fear of death led consumers to online stores (Lavuri, 2021). The threat environment created by the virus does not only meet the basic needs of consumers, but also education, entertainment, business etc. forced their activities and even their socialization needs to be online (Gupta et al., 2021). This situation has made home the focal point for people's needs such as work, rest, education or socialization. In fact, despite the reduction of restrictions, the home remains the center of all activities for many consumers (Accesture, 2020). Of course, this situation has brought along many new needs such as maintaining social ties that have decreased because of social distancing, maintaining existing jobs or meeting educational needs. For this reason, the pandemic period has increased the demand for communication technologies and therefore electronic materials (Kirk & Rifkin, 2020).

Internet service is one of the increasing needs during the pandemic period. Because during the Covid period, when billions of people stayed at home, social interaction between people took place largely through the internet. This development led to great increases in the use of the internet and social media. This advanced social media experience during the Covid 19 pandemic period allowed people to follow the crisis directly and strongly. Naturally, the emotional reactions of this experience were also stronger (Islam et al., 2021). In addition, these reactions were not limited to the experiences of consumers in their own country. Because consumers, who can reach different country experiences thanks to social media, perceived the developments in these countries as a sign of possible policies in their own countries (Keane & Neal, 2021). In this respect, information on the pandemic during the Covid period has become global thanks to social media.

As a result, the pandemic affected all individuals in the world to a greater or lesser extent. This effect had an impact on the consumption behavior of individuals. While people all over the world share the fear and panic caused by the pandemic, the reactions to this issue contain more similarities than differences between countries (Islam et al., 2021). In this context, the reactions of consumer behavior in the face of the pandemic are summarized in the Swiss RE research within the framework of five main trends as follows (Puttaiah et al., 2020):

- Increased digital adoption: People are switching to digital platforms for their daily needs.
- Change in mobility models: Less use of public transport, more remote work, etc.
- Change in purchasing behavior: Online shopping and purchasing for basic needs.
- Increased health awareness: Wearing masks, increased hygiene, healthy eating, etc.
- Changes in interpersonal behavior: Increasing divorce, increasing pet adoption, etc.

The Phase of Coping with the Pandemic

As we have stated before, the Covid 19 pandemic has affected all people to a greater or lesser extent. As it is known, there will be a reaction that develops in return for an effect. In this respect, people started to react to the pandemic and its effects after a while. Naturally, these reactions will be shaped within the framework of many areas according to income, geographical region, or cultural elements (Ellison et al., 2021). In this respect, coping behaviors for the pandemic may differ in many countries. However, the common point here is that people operate the adaptation mechanism as time passes after the initial pandemic shock. Already as the initial shock of the crisis wears off, evidence shows that people are becoming more optimistic (PWC, 2020).

Although the crisis that emerged during the first period of the pandemic was great, the reactions of the people were also very fast. According to the studies of Keane and Neal, the announcement of internal movement restrictions created a significant consumer panic in the short term, but this effect largely disappeared between a week and 10 days (Keane & Neal, 2021). Akhtar et al. also emphasize that the psychological reactance of consumers shows positive resistance to pandemic persuasion. This means that consumers resist temporary threats (Akhtar et al., 2020). Naturally, resistance to threats leads people to seek solutions and accelerates the adaptation process to the pandemic. Thus, people who develop an adaptation strategy over time develop their own coping strategies for working within constraints (Guthrie et al., 2021). In addition, with the emergence of the pandemic, while the consumer welfare fell to its lowest level, it is seen that it improves as the pandemic decreases. This development is partly due to the consumers' adaptation to the situation (Zheng et al., 2021). Naturally, these developments are also reflected in their consumption behaviors.

In this period, there are many different consumer behaviors such as realizing previous behaviors in a virtual dimension (such as virtual chat, virtual fitness activities, etc.), adopting a pet to meet social commitment, developing DIY projects (cooking or gardening, etc.). (Kirk & Rifkin, 2020). However, at this point, the factors that cause great changes in the lives of consumers also lead to differentiation in consumption behaviors. Because in times of crisis, the consumer may try to cope with the negative psychological situation in question by avoiding the elements that will remind him of the trauma he has experienced or by attaching to the elements he has taken shelter in during the trauma period. This, in turn, may cause consumers to reevaluate their priorities and change their consumption behavior (Mathur et al., 2006). For example, the use of the internet and social media has increased during the period when people were under closure due to the pandemic. In this case, interactions in social media have led to differentiation in the purchasing behavior of consumers. (Islam et al., 2021). The most important reflection of this differentiation is the increasing use of social media and the shift of some of the consumers to online shopping instead of physical shopping.

New Normal Phase

Individuals who are faced with a great social trauma first face a shock wave, as we have stated before. After this shock, as individuals adapt to the situation, the situation we call the new normal emerges. In this respect, it is likely that any of the new behaviors adopted by consumers during the pandemic will become the new normal (Goswami & Chouhan, 2021). There are three possible factors that lead to the new normal due to new consumption habits (Sheth, 2020):

- Public Policy: The public's discouragement or encouragement of any consumption may create new consumption habits.
- Technology: Change in technology can create a new normal that will turn requests into needs.
- Changing demographic structure: Changes such as the aging of the population can create new normal due to their new needs.

It can be said that each of these three factors that can create new normal during the Covid pandemic period has a share in the change (even if their weights are different). Of course, the first and most important share is naturally the influence of the public. Because of the public sanctions during the pandemic period, consumers have rediscovered their homes and home life. Socializing at home or working from home has been adopted by many people during the pandemic period, and this has started to be preferred despite the development of public sanctions (Accenture, 2020). Elements such as home life and working from home have also led to differences in consumption behaviors. For example, while the element of eating away from home decreased in food purchasing behavior, transport orders increased (Ellison et al., 2021). Consumers who prefer to cook more at home have begun to fill larger baskets (PWC, 2020). On the other hand, it also reduced food waste by developing behaviors such as preparing grocery lists or using leftover meals for other meals during the pandemic (Vargas-Lopez et al., 2021). An increasing trend in food shopping has been online shopping. There was a 23 % increase in internet shopping transactions worldwide during the pandemic period (Credit Union Magazine, 2020). In fact, internet shopping was on the rise even before the Covid-19 outbreak. The epidemic has increased this structural change (Kim, 2020). According to the study conducted by the international consultancy company Capgemini, 59 % of consumers preferred physical stores before the epidemic, while this rate decreased to 24 % in the current period. However, this rate is expected to increase to 39 % after 6–9 months. On the other hand, while 30 % of consumers preferred internet shopping before the epidemic, this rate increased to 37 % in the current period. For the next 6–9 months, 40 % of consumers are expected to prefer online shopping (Figure 1.3).

Similarly, PWC survey results expect most city dwellers who shop online to continue to do so. However, this does not mean that physical shopping stores will be closed. In this respect, in the future, retail companies will have to combine physical and online store shopping and make multi-channel deliveries (Sheth, 2020). In addition, new sales strategies will change the processes of companies such as new supply and stock.

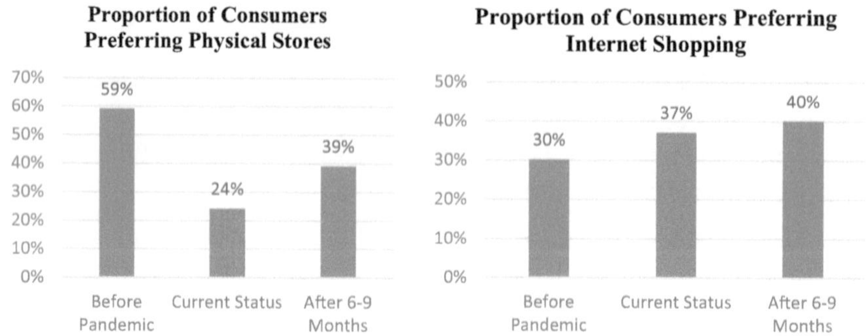

Figure 1.3: The Impact of Covid-19 on Consumers' Preference for Physical Store and Internet Shopping
Source: (Capgemini, 2020:2)

Although online shopping, which leads to changes in consumers' shopping habits, develops with public restrictions, the main reason for this development is the availability of appropriate technology. In this respect, technological development is the reason for the fundamental change in the food shopping of consumers. But the impact of technology on consumer behavior is not limited to this. Developing technology has also contributed to consumers in terms of work, study and leisure time (Eger et al., 2021). Affordable and accessible entertainment activities (such as Netflix, Disney) (Sheth, 2020) and social the technological development that presents it as easier communication in life also supports home life and consumption patterns related to it. In this respect, developing technologies contribute to meeting needs such as belonging, community or status as well as basic needs (Kirk & Rifkin, 2020).

All these developments require that consumer behavior will be different in the future and companies should adapt to it. In response to consumer groups that use and are affected by more social media, their companies will need to increase their digital capabilities (Gupta et al., 2021). In addition, companies should focus on providing quality experience to consumers in trauma situations and continue their promotional activities (Pantanovd., 2021). Because the change in consumer behavior in the future will radically change the supply, stock and sales strategies of companies. In this respect, in the process that will lead to creative destruction, companies that can adapt to this will survive, while others will shrink or must withdraw from the market.

Table 1.2: Economic growth in some selected regions (%)

	2019	2020	2021 (Expectation)
Earth	2.8	−3.1	5.9
Developed countries	1.7	−4.5	5.2
USA	2.2	−3.4	6.0
EU	1.3	−6.3	5.0
Developing countries	3.7	−2.1	6.4
Turkey	0.9	1.8	9.0
Russia	1.3	−3.0	4.7
Chinese	6.1	2.3	8.0
India	4.2	−7.3	9.5

Source: IMF, World Economic Outlook, October 2021 and October 2020.

General Trend in Consumer Spending in Turkey

The pandemic has affected all countries to a greater or lesser extent. Social restrictions during the pandemic period had negative effects on the country's economies. In this respect, as can be seen from Table 1.2, the pandemic has had negative effects on economic growth all over the world. While the economy experienced a shrinkage of 3.1 % throughout the world, this rate was 4.5 % in developed countries. On the other hand, although developing countries were adversely affected by the pandemic, it performed better than developing countries.

While almost all countries experienced negative growth during the pandemic period, Turkey has been one of the few countries in the world that achieved growth. This does not mean that Turkey has not been affected by the pandemic at all. We will use card expenditure data in the study to see the domestic demand in Turkey during the pandemic period. Although not all expenditures are made with cards, card expenditure data is important in terms of showing the general trend in country expenditures. Turkey's increasing export performance during the pandemic period has been the most important factor bringing growth. When we look at the rate of change in card expenditures in Turkey in real prices to see the change in domestic demand, it is possible to see that expenditures have increased in 2020 as well (Chart 1). This outlook shows that consumers in Turkey are not as pessimistic about the future during the pandemic as in the rest of the world. However, this does not mean that Turkey and consumers in Turkey are not affected by the pandemic, as we have stated before.

Figure 1.4 shows the change in card shopping in Turkey by months. As can be seen from the graph, the pandemic process had a significant impact on the

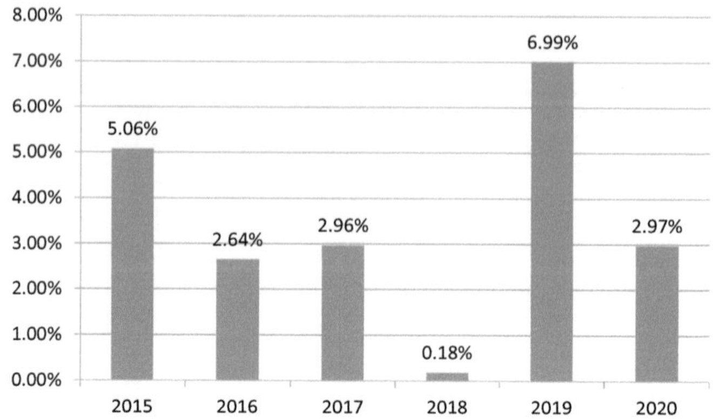

Figure 1.4: Change of Card Real Expenditures by Years in Turkey %
Source: Prepared using Interbank Card Center data.

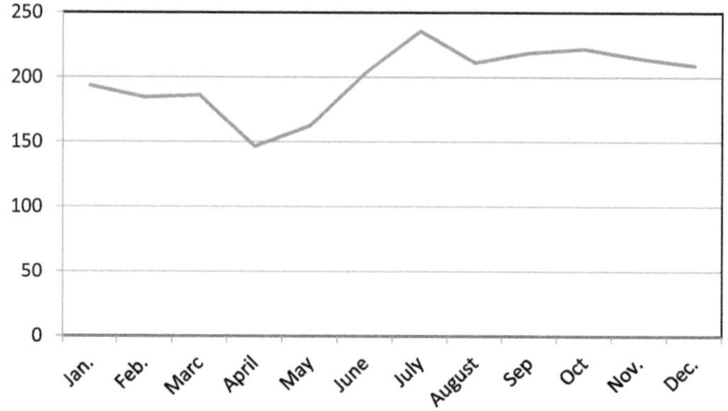

Figure 1.5 : The Amount of Real Card Shopping in Turkey by Month in 2020 (Million TL)
Source: Prepared using data from Interbank Card Center and TUIK.

expenditures made. It is possible to explain this effect with the RCA model, namely react – cope – adapt stages. The shock that occurred with the restriction decision of the public authority as a result of the increase in the number of cases in the fourth month, created a significant decrease in expenditures and formed the react phase. The reaction at this stage is due to the fact that households reduce their expenditures due to concerns about the future. Afterwards, the coping phase takes place until the seventh month, and at this stage, the desire to get rid of the effects of the crisis is reflected as an increase in consumers' expenditures. In the new normal phase that occurs after the seventh month, it is possible to see that the expenditures enter a horizontal trend. As can be seen from the model, although there is no decrease in consumer spending in Turkey in 2020, the effect of the pandemic is clearly seen throughout the year.

Another table where we can see the effect of the pandemic is Table 1.3, which shows which sectors 100 units of money are spent in Turkey in the first 9 months of 2020. The item that we can see the effect of the pandemic most clearly in the table is the grocery and food shopping item. and biological needs. In this sense, market-food expenditures are directed to the first part of the pyramid of needs. In this context, while food shopping was in the band of 30 units in the first months, it reached approximately 42 units in April with the increase of the pandemic. After the initial shock, it decreased in the adaptation period, while the new normally regressed almost to the old level. There are two sectors that attract the main attention in the table. The first of these is the airline – travel item. Because, as consumers begin to grapple with uncertainties during the pandemic process, their purchasing behavior becomes even more ambiguous and indecisive. In this respect, consumers tend to reduce their spending on all products and services that they deem almost unnecessary in the "dark future" (Vatandaş, 2020).

In fact, this development, which has occurred in many sectors, has developed somewhat differently in airline – travel expenses. Because in the first months of 2020, approximately 3 % of consumer expenditures were made in this sector, while in the period that we will describe as the new normal after the shock, unlike many sectors, expenditures still could not return to their old level. In this, the ongoing travel restrictions of public authorities at many points may have a share, as well as the delay of consumers' hedonic needs due to the increasing fear of disease during the pandemic period. The second sector that draws attention in the table is the electronic – computer shopping item. With the pandemic process, the emergence of options such as working from home or shopping remotely, electronic explains the increase in expenditures. However, after the shock, the share of this item in expenditures increased from 5 % to 8 %. In addition to the online education, the concept of working from home, which is now the new reality of our lives, may have a share in this increase.

Another expenditure item that supports the idea that home and home life has come to a very central point in people's lives is the expenditures for building materials. It is in question that these expenditures, which fall into the second region of the pyramid of needs, for security needs, have increased compared to the first situation in the post-crisis period. In this context, expenditures on

Table 1.3: Distribution of 100 TL real spending in Turkey by sectors on a monthly basis

	Jan.	Feb.	Marc.	Apr.	May	June	July	Aug.	Sep.
Market- Food-Various Food	29,09	30,49	36,30	41,80	37,20	33,13	31,53	31,93	31,74
Liquid fuel	7,19	6,90	7,10	5,91	5,61	6,71	7,29	7,88	6,95
Clothing -Accessory	8,23	7,82	5,37	3,25	5,22	7,10	7,60	6,48	6,49
Electronic-Computer	5,08	5,41	5,75	7,77	8,57	8,24	6,88	7,39	8,20
Airline-Travel	3,01	2,96	1,48	0,17	0,40	0,95	1,50	1,68	1,48
Insurance	4,05	3,95	4,32	4,50	4,22	4,42	3,90	3,52	3,75
Construction materials	4,16	4,59	5,14	5,34	5,60	6,12	5,66	5,58	5,92
Furniture-Decoration	2,75	2,97	2,83	2,59	3,31	3,99	3,53	3,38	3,37
Health -Cosmetics	4,26	4,43	4,49	3,33	3,40	3,94	3,73	3,88	4,20
Telecommunication	2,60	2,55	2,66	2,99	2,77	2,43	2,31	2,21	2,21
Education-Stationery	6,41	6,62	5,55	4,90	4,73	4,78	5,37	5,34	6,65
Accomodation	4,57	4,25	2,67	0,93	1,01	1,96	3,46	4,46	3,31
Jewelers	1,76	2,62	1,29	0,56	0,84	1,04	1,32	1,44	1,35
Tax	4,90	2,08	2,31	3,06	3,88	2,98	4,46	2,99	2,19
BES	0,83	0,84	0,89	1,10	1,01	0,79	0,71	0,71	0,73
Other	11,12	11,51	11,83	11,80	12,23	11,45	10,76	11,12	11,48

Source: Prepared using BKM data.

building materials have increased from 4 % to about 6 %. In other words, with the increasing home life, it is possible for people to spend more on their homes, which are their safe zones, during the pandemic period.

Online Consumer Spending in Turkey

One of the areas where the pandemic process has caused a great development is online shopping. Especially during the intense periods of the pandemic, online shopping triggered by the increasing fear and uncertainty environment has shown a significant increase in Turkey as well as in the whole world. As can be seen in Figure 1.6 below, the expenditures made over the internet with domestic cards increased by 60 % on an annual basis in 2020 compared to months. But

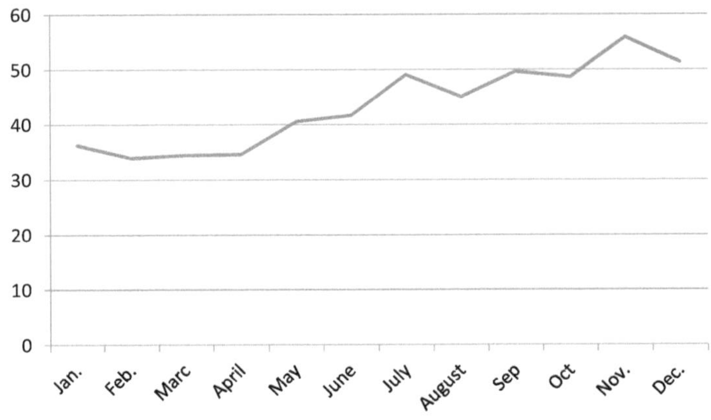

Figure 1.6: The Real Amount of Online Shopping with Domestic Cards in Turkey in 2020 by Month (Million TL)

Source: Interbank Card Center.

more importantly, the increase that occurred during the first outbreak of the pandemic continues afterward. In this respect, it would not be wrong to say that online shopping will be the first among the new normal of the world after the pandemic.

When we look at the sectoral distribution of expenditures made over the Internet, a structure like the general spending trend emerges. While food and electronics – computer expenditures are the sectors with the greatest increase, airline – travel is the sector with the highest decrease in expenditures. But many sectors have been affected by the online shopping wind. In this respect, it will not be unexpected that online shopping will gain strength in the future. However, this does not mean that physical shopping will decrease. Hybrid structures that combine physical and online shopping seem possible in response to the increasing online shopping in the future.

Conclusion

When we look at the effects of the pandemic process on consumers in Turkey, the first thing that stands out is the increase in consumption expenditures in 2020. This outlook shows that consumers in Turkey are not as pessimistic about the future during the pandemic as in the rest of the world. However, this does not mean that consumers in Turkey are not affected by the pandemic. When we

Table 1.4: Distribution of real spending of 100 TL on the Internet in Turkey on a monthly basis by sector

	Jan.	Feb.	Marc.	Apr.	May	June	July	Aug.	Sep.
Market- Food-Various Food	7,24	9,15	12,35	15,50	13,59	12,68	10,65	11,61	12,02
Liquid fuel	3,12	3,26	3,19	2,61	1,96	2,86	3,29	3,43	3,15
Clothing-Accessory	6,77	7,13	6,41	8,32	8,61	7,30	5,93	5,79	7,02
Electronic-Computer	11,94	13,13	16,30	23,56	23,83	20,41	15,92	17,32	19,34
Airline-Travel	13,04	12,90	6,34	0,58	1,35	4,04	6,28	6,70	5,54
Construction materials	5,48	6,38	7,81	6,46	6,57	8,84	8,21	8,55	8,59
Furniture-Decoration	1,84	2,33	2,71	3,14	3,19	3,30	2,71	2,76	2,73
Health-Cosmetics	1,78	1,95	2,38	2,26	2,11	1,94	1,49	1,57	1,66
Telecommunication	4,94	4,98	5,39	5,34	4,56	4,54	4,43	4,47	4,33
Education-Stationery	6,83	8,45	7,08	6,45	6,06	6,25	8,50	8,14	11,03
Accomodation	8,03	7,41	4,34	0,73	1,01	3,18	6,12	5,77	3,70
jewelers	0,15	0,22	0,19	0,22	0,30	0,16	0,15	0,17	0,15
Tax	13,93	5,75	7,56	8,85	10,66	8,57	12,23	8,47	5,47
Other	14,93	16,96	17,94	15,98	16,21	15,91	14,09	15,25	15,26

Source: Prepared using BKM data.

look at the consumption expenditures monthly in 2020, it is seen that it is in a structure in accordance with the RCA model, and although there was a decrease in consumption expenditures during the first crisis phase, a rapid adaptation period followed.

The pandemic period has initiated many changes in both the general structure of consumption expenditures and sectoral basis in Turkey as well as in the whole world. Changing consumer behavior will radically change the supply, stock and sales strategies of companies. In this respect, creative destruction is inevitable. In short, we will have to get used to the "new normal" at many points in the future. Because companies that can adapt to this process, both in Turkey and in the world, will survive while others will shrink or must withdraw from the market. In this respect, it will be much more beneficial both economically and socially for companies to focus on the opportunities created by moving away from the concerns brought by the crisis.

İ. Burçak Vatansever Durmaz

Chapter 2 The Big Reset in Human Resources Systems

Introduction

Increasing the efficiency while decreasing the costs is one of the most important issues in terms of companies since the 1st Industrial Revolution. Managerial theories suggested by Henry Ford and Frederick Taylor have been implemented by companies to rise the efficiency in whole of the corporate activities and functions. In this regard, new tools, new ways for the production and working, and new technologies have been sought and investigated in the process after 1st Industrial Revolution (Drucker, 1999). These new ways, tools and technologies have shaped following industrial revolutions around the world in time. And lastly, 4th Industrial Revolution was announced by German government in 2011. While autonomous systems are in the basis of 3rd Industrial Revolution, the driving force of 4th Industrial Revolution has been accepted as the cyber-physical systems (Bartodziej, 2015). These industrial revolutions have also affected human resources management systems in the companies. In this respect, works based on labor power have started to be disappeared, and works based on brain power and machines have risen. Thus, a vital shift from labor-focused works to information-focused works has emerged for years (Handy, 1984).

In this chapter, the big reset in human resources systems in companies is explained. In this regard, changing role of human resources in companies, changes in the human resources management with Industry 4.0, effects of digital transformation on human resources management, artificial intelligence and its effects on human resources management, and the big reset in human resources management functions due to Industry 4.0, digital transformation and artificial intelligence are mentioned in this chapter.

Changing Role of Human Resources Management

Human resources are one of the most important and valuable resources of companies in today's conditions. Previously, employees did monotonic jobs in limited and certain working styles and conditions. However, today employees are individuals who are involved in business development processes of the companies, make positive contributions to the employer, determine the problems and make analyses, and give advices for the solutions of business problems (Nerdrum & Erikson, 2001).

To gain competitive advantage in a market by a company, its most important resource is known as the human resource today, because human resource of a company provides an economic basis to investigate the competitive advantage of the company in the market (Barney, 1991). In this regard, first, the changing definition of the human resource management should be made. In 1980s, human resources management was defined as a strategical approach about the employment and development of qualified labor power who are committed to the job in the company in order to reach into the corporate goals (Hecklau et al., 2016). Today, in the broadest sense, human resources management is a consistent and strategical approach developed to manage the human effectively who is the most valuable asset of an organization (Pellegrini, Rizzi & Frey, 2018). Hence, organizations using the human resources effectively and efficiently would become much successful than the rivals, although these rivals' capitals, raw materials and other important production factors are similar with the organization. Moreover, it can be claimed that all small, medium and large companies should manage their human resources effectively in order to reach into the achievement in the market. In this way, productivity of the organizations might also increase. Since effective human resources management make the employees satisfied, these satisfied employees can make more effort for qualified production. Thus, such an effort can bring the success for the organization (Treven, 2000).

To gain competitive advantage, organization should use their all resources effectively. After accepting the human is one of the most important parts in the production, human factor creates a new field within the scope of studies focused on optimizing resource efficiency, because human can create unique opportunities for the organizations in the rising competition besides it is an important resources for the production. Today, it is seen that human resource is one of the important parts of companies' intellectual capitals such as patents, copyrights, brand equities and etc. (Burma, 2014).

Industry 4.0 and Human Resources Management

Since the beginning of industrialization process, there have been paradigm changes in the industry due to technological changes and innovations. These paradigm changes are known as industrial revolutions. The paradigms that were changed in the industrial revolutions are mechanization in 1st Industrial Revolution, high use of electricity energy in 2nd Industrial Revolution, and electronic and automation in 3rd Industrial Revolution (Shamim et al., 2016).

These three industrial revolutions had lasted almost 200 years. Firstly, steam engines started the 1st Industrial Revolution in 1780s, and it brought a huge increase in the productivity and efficiency. Second Industrial Revolution began after 100 years of 1st Industrial Revolution with the discover of division of labor and production line system, and this system had increased the productivity and efficiency again. Third Industrial Revolution emerged in 1970s with developed modern automation systems which brought flexibility and increased efficiency in the production (Drath & Horch, 2014).

In 2011, 4th Industrial Revolution which is a complex system involving digital production, Internet communication, computer and automation technologies, smart factories, smart machines and etc., has started (Nunes, Pereira & Alves, 2017). Industry 4.0 promises low costs, high quality and efficiency and customer satisfaction for companies in global competition (Wamba et al., 2015).

Industry 4.0 to be widespread brings a rapid change in working life (Zhong et al., 2017). It is forecasted that the need for labor power in production sector would be reshaped, and the needed individual abilities and capabilities would become diversified (Bonekamp & Sure, 2015). In this regard, it is predicted that the working life, office hours, remote working, part-time working, company structures and etc. would change in the near future (Haijan & Fangfang, 2018).

Organizations were developed via strategical approaches emerged from previous industrial revolutions, and thus, a shift from personnel management into human resources management appeared in the organizations (Caruso, 2018). In this regard, existing labor power need has started to change quantitatively and qualitatively (Mihalcea, 2017). Furthermore, human factor became the center of production with Industry 4.0. In case of any need, employees would become involved in automation systems, and there would be much need for human power in order to solve the complex problems (Morrar, Arman & Mousa, 2017).

Industry 4.0 would influence evaluation styles of human resources management departments about the tendencies related to human (Liboni et al., 2019), because it can be claimed that the field of human resources management has been rapidly changed and developed with the increasing technology. In this regard, Industry 4.0 technologies require various radical changes in human resources management departments (Armstrong & Taylor, 2014).

Essentially human resources management makes important contribution for companies in terms of Industry 4.0 process within the scope of employees to be recruited, trained and developed. When taking into consideration that technological developments result in increasing digitalization and automation, complexity of the processes rises, and new business models emerge. As the result, the structure and content of the workplaces are changing. Moreover, operations are supported by cyber-physical systems more, and in what degree the network would be used by human-machine interaction is based on technological, economical and corporate conditions (Fettig et al., 2018). Furthermore, it is seen that organizations spend so much money to store and manage the data about the human resource due to the lack of network equipment. Therefore, it is asserted that accepting the technology in human resources management would decrease the gap between the technology and human factor (Marvel et al., 2016).

Digital Transformation and its Effects on Human Resources Management

Globalization affects both employees, organizations and human resources management individually, organizationally and economically, and brings various new opportunities. Eliminating the barriers about information share globally in information society era influences organizations and business processes positively (McKinsey & Company, 2017). In this respect, digital transformation and digital technologies appear. Digital transformation enabling direct communication of companies with their target customers, has provided a variety of media channels, generated more accurate content for target customers, and generated new areas of expertise (Dietrich & Livingston, 2012).

Digital technologies enable lots of jobs made by human manually to be done autonomously, thus these make possible to do the same production via employing less personnel. In this regard, it can be claimed that digitalization would increase the unemployment when ignoring the economical contribution of digital transformation. It is predicted that 50 % of existing jobs can be made via digitalized automation technologies theoretically (McKinsey, 2017).

Information technologies are used by human resources management departments in information era to gather, archive, correct, analyze, and share the data and information. Via the resources brought by the technology, human resources management departments have become strategic planners from a non-managerial statue and managed to affect personnel at the management level with the information sources it provided (Greengard, 1994).

Human resources management professionals who work digitally in the department and have an important role for the organization's other departments to become digital. If human resources management professionals discover new technologies, platforms and working ways, digital transformation process starts in human resources management. In this respect, Jain (2018) explains the digital transformation process in human resources management field as followings:

a. *Redescribing Policies*: The role of today's human resources management should be defined as a team helping the management and employees to adapt into the way of digital thinking rapidly. Thus, information should be gained about organization structures connected to the network, corporate network analysis and digital leadership models.
b. *Coordinating The Mix Labor Power*: The teams should be determined to discover and set up new supplier solutions, and artificial intelligence solutions should be evaluated for recruitment and developing the learning. The focus point here should be to use integrated power and abilities of a different labor power rather than managing the processes.
c. *Increasing Main Core Technology*: Old digital systems should be changed with an appropriate platform for a strong digital infrastructure. Old systems used for learning, recruitment and performance management should be upgraded and the systems that can be easily used by the employees should be used.
d. *Creating A Digital Human Resources Management Team*: Human resources management should be organized with powerful business partners according to field of specializations. Organization model of human resources management should reshape in order to focus on efforts about employee experience, analytics, culture and new learning world.
e. *MakingInnovationMainStrategyinHumanResourcesManagement*:Innovations should be made about performance management applications. Novelties such as using the data about finding individuals during recruitment process who have high performance should be discovered in the companies.
f. *Higher Process Automation*: Technology platforms and processes strengthening the managers in order to maximize the performance, satisfaction and participation of employees should be implemented.
g. *Directing New Individuals to Human Resources Management Occupation*: Individuals should be regularly canalized into human resources management from workplace. Moreover, innovation teams should be generated, and new abilities should be gained to them by top-level managers via mentoring them.
h. *Benchmarking*: Other companies should be visited to see what they do. Moreover, human resources management professionals can bring some experts for workshops and seminars, take part in research membership programs, and seek for new ideas continuously to encourage innovativeness.

Artificial Intelligence and Human Resources Management

Artificial intelligence is defined as rationally acting systems thinking and acting like human rationally (Russel & Norwig, 2010). Moreover, artificial intelligence can be described as the intelligence displayed by machines in contrast to the natural intelligence displayed by human (Jain, 2018). Artificial intelligence is a discipline aiming at understanding natural intelligence in the designing process of computer programs imitating human intelligence. In this regard, the goal of artificial intelligence is to think and act like human (Nabiyev, 2012). Furthermore, there are some important dimensions of artificial intelligence which are reasoning, information display, automatic planning and scheduling, machine learning, natural language processing, artificial vision, robotics, and artificial general or super intelligence (Staub et al., 2015).

Brynjolfsion and McAfee (2011) stated that a new industrial revolution has started with using artificial intelligence in all departments, and types of doing jobs would change. Human resources management professionals have discovered advantages of data-focused effective decision-making today. As data-focused technologies and artificial intelligence analyze gigantic data stack to predict the disposition and provide some advice and forecast the information from this data stack. Artificial intelligence can help human resources management professionals to discover the human resource better through using labor force data of organization, and to predict the problems and dispositions (Merlin & Jayam, 2018).

Nowadays, human resources management divisions have the tendency to set up digital transformation and use some techniques to make simple the resources through using the big data analysis, artificial intelligence, cloud computing and more. Lots of companies use artificial intelligence and other digital technologies such as chatbot, machine learning and robot processing automation that provide supports for chatting, scanning, job orientation programs, interviews and etc. (Yawalkar, 2019).

Artificial intelligence assists human resources division to realize the cognitive science and cognitive modelling. Moreover, it includes effective analysis of the facts in the past time, present time, and future time. Investigating past facts is entitled "reporting", investigating present facts is entitled "analysis", and investigating future facts is entitled "foresighted analysis" (Jain, 2017).

Artificial intelligence that is used in human resources division diminishes the burden about administrative employees in working place, enable true employee candidates to be preferred for the job position, help the personnel to get various new capabilities, and help to predict the retention rate of personnel. Moreover, these applications help minimizing the errors, workflow to be retained in various departments, personnel to participate more, and prejudice acts to be diminished during decision-making (Yawalkar, 2019).

In recent future period, it is predicted that computer and machine performance would exceed the human performance. In this regard, employees should hold themselves in readiness for some important changes for human performance to compete with machine and computer performance. The "to-do-list" for white-collar employees in this process can be stated as follows (KPMG, 2017):

a. White-collar employees should not be afraid of moving the house for new job opportunities, and they should be open to replace the city, even the country.
b. They can gain new abilities and capabilities. Individuals who are open for learning would win always.
c. Individuals approaching to the developments with suspicion or who avoid from developing have difficulties to find a job.
d. Individuals acting flexible and adapting into the changes in the economy would keep pace with the big change much easier.
e. Individuals who are calm and solution-oriented against the problems would have advantage than their rivals.
f. Human who is smart that can create the artificial intelligence, could protect, even increase the welfare level for both existing and further generations via the ability of creativity and adaptability.
g. Innovation creates new innovations. The important thing here is to have the vision to create these innovations.

Tambe et al. (2019) stated that artificial intelligence is required, beneficial and inevitable for human resources management departments. In this regard, Tambe et al. (2019) expressed the potential effects of artificial intelligence on human resources management as follows:

a. Artificial intelligence might increase the operational efficiency in human resources management department.
b. Artificial intelligence might help human resources management professionals to make rapid decisions.
c. Artificial intelligence might decrease the costs in human resources management department via automatic scanning applications.
d. Artificial intelligence might provide better employee experience.
e. Artificial intelligence might increase employees' learning and development capacity in training and development process.

f. Artificial intelligence might organize the wages during wage management process.
g. Artificial intelligence might improve performance evaluation systems of managers.
h. Artificial intelligence might strengthen employees' abilities such as adaptation, problem solving, interaction, emotional intelligence, creativity, leadership, risk management, intrapreneurship, overcoming the stress and etc.
i. Artificial intelligence might identify weaknesses of the employees correctly.
j. Artificial intelligence might provide quick feedback to managers and employees.
k. Artificial intelligence might provide the managers to realize qualified employees quickly.
l. Artificial intelligence might make the working process simple.
m. Artificial intelligence might activate managers' decision processes.
n. Employees might think that the justice is developed via using artificial intelligence technologies in the organization.
o. Artificial intelligence might help the employees to strengthen their social interactions via providing them leisure time.
p. Artificial intelligence might increase the possibility that the human resources management department fulfil its targets.
q. Human resources management department managers might less meet with risky situations due to artificial intelligence practices.
r. Artificial intelligence might reshape the talent management process.
s. Artificial intelligence algorithms might provide recommendations about learning programs of the labor power in the organization.

The Big Reset in Human Resources Management Functions

Human resources practice consists of the time from the employee candidate to participates in the organization to leave the job. In general, human resources management processes can be sorted as recruitment, selection, training and development, performance evaluation, career management, and wage management (Schuler & Jackson, 1987).

Recruitment

Recruitment means the process of finding suitable employee candidates that the organization needs (Hom et al., 1999). In recruitment function of human resources management, artificial intelligence can be used today. Before using artificial intelligence, it was so time-consuming to investigate thousands of CVs, and make decision on suitable candidates during recruitment process. However, human resources management personnel can enter some important criteria such as experience, age, foreign language, education and etc. for the job in a computer program via artificial intelligence technologies, and the CVs of all candidates can be filtered rapidly according to these pre-determined criteria (Chang, 2009). After filtration, the program generates short lists in which most suitable candidates for the job are written. Then, Chatbot is used for preselection which enables human resources management to communicate with the candidate. Chatbot gives 7/24 support to human resources management professionals, help for big data pool to be generated for decision-making processes in human resources management to be much objective, and presents the results of preselection to human resources management professionals. And the program (Chatbot) gives information about the situation of the application of the candidates to them (Eubanks, 2019).

Companies like Scholastic Aptitude Test, Facebook, General Electric benefits from digital technologies during recruitment in scanning for new talents, making interviews, identifying and etc. Recruitment manager evaluates candidates' applications easily through artificial intelligence programs, and candidates could gain answers from the company rapidly in a short time (Yawalkar, 2019).

Selection

Candidate selection process starts with constituting the candidate pool and determining the qualifications and features of the employee who would be employed in the organization. Then, inappropriate candidates are eliminated from the candidate pool. In this preselection process, personal information, job manners and education of the candidates are examined. In case of the candidate's features and qualifications is suitable with the job, this candidate is included into final selection pool. After passing preselection, candidates fill the detailed application form; thus, the candidate can be much comprehensively evaluated. After the phase of filling the application form, some tests were made on candidates to measure their abilities, capabilities, and knowledge such as intelligence test, ability test, information test, perception test, personality test and etc. These tests analyze the harmony between the candidate, and the needs of working place and job. According to these tests, the suitable employee profile is determined (Bretz & Judge, 1998).

Selecting the most suitable, qualified, and right employee for the job position is one of the most costly and difficult phases in the human resources management process. Wrong decisions on employing a candidate or wrong recruitment process could rise the turnover rate of employees in the company and generate significant loss of time and money for the company. For example, interviews made with the candidates could be influenced by some subjective elements and enables the decision-maker of human resources management department. Nowadays, artificial intelligence's use during selection step enables the work of decision-makers easier and enables them to make the right selection. Final decision is made by human power; however, artificial intelligence guides them to identify and match the criteria on candidates who are appropriate for the job and brings timesaving in the selection phase (Murgai, 2018).

When evaluating the big reset in recruitment and selection process of human resources management, computers started to be used in recruitment in 1970, ERP system began to be used in 1979, developed web-based system started to be used in 1990, cloud-based human resources management solution was launched in 2006, video recruitment system started to be used in 2016, and big data analysis began to be used in 2017 (Onik, Miraz & Kim, 2018).

During video interview evaluation, artificial intelligence focuses on 25,000 different data points, and scans candidates' various features and complex relations among these features. Tone of voice, mimics, jests and micro expressions of the candidate in the interview are so important here. In fact, candidates are investigated in terms of many features that cannot be identified by any qualified human resources expert. In this regard, artificial intelligence can analyze whether the candidate lies, and the candidate is stressful (Lu et al., 2018).

Training and Development

Training and development are related to changes in the behaviors. Training is mostly about doing the jobs, while development focuses on individuals working in the organization (Man, 2017). If organizations desire to benefit from their employees effectively, organizations should train and develop them (Arthur et al., 2003).

After recruitment and selection process, the most suitable candidates transform into employees of the organization. For the adaptation of these employees to the job and organization, and in order to transfer the required information about the job to the employees training programs are organized. Today, thanks to Industry 4.0, these training programs can be made via robotics technologies. Robot instructors might behave like human, might identify voices and images, and even discuss on world problems and offer solutions (Ford, 2018). To adopt the industry 4.0 and digital transformation successfully, organizations should re-educate their labor power, and training systems should try to fill the gap in the abilities about information and communication technologies (Lorenz et al., 2015).

Some elements of training phase might be also automated with the help of machine learning. Association rules mining has helped in automating the detection of personnel' training needs and the recommendation of relevant courses for them. IBM as a technology company is supporting some huge companies like Royal Bank of Scotland in installing Chatbot that serves as individual career advisors for the personnel and recommend relevant trainings and readings (Garg et al., 2021).

Performance Evaluation

Performance management emerges due to the desire for systematic planning, and desire to reach into individual and organizational goals. Performance evaluation aims at simultaneous or periodical success evaluation about the individual and organizational goals (Strohmeier & Piazza, 2015). Performance evaluation system which is suitable to Industry 4.0 should focus on the development of the employees, result-oriented approach and behavior-oriented approach, because these approaches can make the learning and innovation much easier (Shamim et al., 2016).

Companies can get so much data about their employees via artificial intelligence technologies, but to get so much data is not so important. The vital thing here is to use this existing data accurately and effectively. Artificial intelligence technologies make a detailed evaluation of every personnel according to the data gained from the employees. As the result of the evaluation, the average performance score is determined. Moreover, the program can predict in which degree the personnel will have a performance in the future. Through such a performance evaluation, the program can easily determine the fields that the employee has some lacks whose performance score is under the average level. Artificial intelligence reports the field that the employee has lacks to the department manager. Thus, whether lack of the employee is filled can be identified via repeated performance evaluations (Eubanks, 2019).

Career Management

The widespread use of computers and Internet in the world in the last years has changed the business life; thus, the central factor identifying the existing employment and career has become the increasing role of technology in the working places. Today, most of the jobs and tasks can be done by machines and robots. In this regard, human must learn to work with these complex machines and robots (Hirschi, 2015).

Artificial intelligence which is a data-based technology extrapolates information form the big data in the organization in order to determine the promotion of the employees, identify the abilities that an employee needs, and provide new ideas. For this purpose, it uses retroactive historical data and predictive analytics. Therefore, it might offer some advice about application and opportunities to the human resources management department (McGovern et al., 2018).

Wage Management

Wage management means employees' wages which include also profit share and retirement plans. Wage management is a complex function in terms of organizations, and there can be sometimes mistakes resulted from human factor in wage management (Strohmeier & Piazza, 2015). However, artificial intelligence extinguishes traditional wage system to minimize mistake possibility (Das et al., 2020). Organizations started to overcome physical and time obstacles with digitalization. Via the Industry 4.0, time and space dimensions of the job has changed, and new flexible organizational opportunities have emerged for all labor power. As the result, flexible working hours and remote working have replaced with traditional office hours (Bissola & Imperatori, 2018). Developments in information and communication technologies enables companies to work digitally and remotely, and the use of remote working practice has started to rise especially during Covid-19 process (Eyel, 2021). Moreover, in flexible working, employees can select working days and hours in the week, and when to start and quit to work (Eyel, 2020). Due to these changes in working schedule, determining wages becomes much difficult. In this regard, wage system should be harmonized with flexible working and remote working practices during digital transformation process resulted from Industry 4.0 (Bissola & Imperatori, 2018).

It can be claimed that adopting technology-based systems in wage management diminishes error margin when comparing with traditional wage management systems. In this regard, artificial intelligence technologies started to be used in identifying the wage that would be paid to the employees (Wang, 2019). In traditional wage management system, the wages of the employees are identified according to their positions, while it is identified according to the employees' abilities and capabilities and their performance results in artificial intelligence (Das et al., 2020).

Conclusion

After the 1st Industrial Revolution appeared in the late 18th century, machines were started to be used in the production process in established huge factories, and both the factory owners and academicians evaluated the machine as the same with the human factor in production process. However, the importance and value of human factor in the production and general organizational functions was realized in the first half of the 20th century. With the modern and post-modern management approaches, human became the main factor in intellectual capital of the organizations, and human resources management departments started to be established in the organizations after 1970s in return for the personnel management departments.

In 1980s, globalization process started, and there emerged lots of developments in information and communication technologies in 1980s, 1990s, and 2000s. After adapting technology into many corporate functions and departments, and with the growth in the companies, there has arisen a need to digitalize the human resources management departments' functions in order to increase the effectiveness and efficiency in these departments. And this practice has brought the "Big Reset" in human resources management.

Today, technological developments due to the industry 4.0, digital transformation, artificial intelligence and etc. bring efficiency and effectiveness in human resources management functions such as recruitment, selection, training and development, performance evaluation, career management, wage management and etc. Thus, organizations adopting and practicing these technologies in their human resources management departments could decrease their costs about human resources and increase the profitability. In conclusion, it can be claimed that the big reset in human relations management would affect all organizations around the world soon, and organizations can adapt into these developments would maintain their sustainable successes; on the other hand, organizations cannot adopt these changes would lose their profitability, market share, their employer brand value would decrease, and their costs would rise.

Sinem Eray

Chapter 3 A 'Great Reset' is Coming, New Capitalism

Introduction

Globalization is primarily concerned with the social and cultural ramifications of today's capitalism. As a result, considering the fundamental characteristics of capitalism can help explain the phenomena of labor transformation in the globalization process.

Although capitalism can be defined in its most basic form as an economic system based on production, the exchange of goods and services, private ownership, and the use of capital to make a large profit, it is a system that pervades and characterizes all aspects of social life, including much more complex processes. Since its inception in Europe in the 16th century, capitalism has been in a perpetual state of mutation and renewal as an economic system that has gradually impacted the entire world. This is not to say, however, that capitalism lacks certain fundamental qualities that have persisted from the past to the present and give it its identity.

In the last two centuries, important intellectual changes have been experienced in our world, and these intellectual changes have brought about great movements. Man's struggle for freedom and attempts to control the social environment continue today, as in the past. Some of the idea systems put forward in this process have created great debates and conflicts. As a matter of fact, the problems created by the concepts discussed in the context of the state, power, society, equality, human rights and freedoms have not lost their currency and do not seem to lose. Some of the most important of these concepts are 'Capitalism' and 'Socialism' that rose in response to it.

The Great Reset is shaped around the main idea of rebuilding the world economy and redesigning capitalism after the Covid-19 pandemic. The concept of "Great Reset", which was put forward by Prince Charles, Prince of Wales, and Klaus Schwab, President of the World Economic Forum, in May 2020, was the main theme of the Virtual Davos meeting held in January 2021. According to those who came up with the idea of the Great Reset, the world is currently experiencing the biggest crisis after the Great Depression in 1929 due to Covid-19. Covid-19 will have very serious and long-term effects on economic growth, public debt, employment and human well-being. With Covid-19, income injustice, environmental problems and economic problems created by capitalism have increased, so it is time to make a new reset to capitalism. According to Schwab, it is possible to transform capitalism through the state, which is more effective and stronger in the Covid-19 process. For a more livable world, it is necessary to renew and transform all the failing aspects of society and economies, from education to social contracts and working conditions, and to act together and quickly in line with this goal. In short, the great reset is expressed not as a transition to a brand new system, but as a restructuring of capitalism and changing its failing aspects (Schwab, 2020a).

The Covid-19 pandemic and the subsequent economic and social crisis that the world fell into have very clearly revealed the vulnerability of health services, social protection, education, value chains, production networks, financial markets, public transport systems and ecosystems in the world. The humanitarian, social and economic impacts of the Covid-19 pandemic have the potential to reverse progress so far in achieving sustainable development goals. For this reason, it is recommended to take collective action to recover from the crisis and manage economic, social and environmental policy objectives in line with sustainable development goals worldwide (OECD, 2020, p. 3).

The Covid-19 process has shown that markets, which are expected to self-manage and solve their problems within themselves, have failed to solve health and epidemic problems without state intervention, and it has dealt a great blow to the neoliberal economy, which has advocated the minimum state understanding from the 1980s to the present. The invisible hand of Adam Smith did not heal the wounds during the pandemic process, so the state, which was wanted to remain at a minimum level according to the neoclassical theory, grew, became smarter and even became an entrepreneurial state that cooperated with the private sector (Mazzucato & Quaggiotto, 2020).

Management consulting firm McKinsey & Company has published a report addressing the issue of stakeholder capitalism, which came to the fore at the Davos Summit, which was held for the fifth time this year. In the report titled "The State of Stakeholder Capitalism", the Founding President of the World Economic Forum, Dr. It was discussed why this concept, which was brought up again by Klaus Schwab years later, was needed. McKinsey shares five principles that will guide companies aiming to achieve stakeholder engagement. These; involve the board of directors, set and follow environmental targets, work for the development of all suppliers, focus on long-term benefit while meeting the needs of consumers, and respect employees and invest in their future.

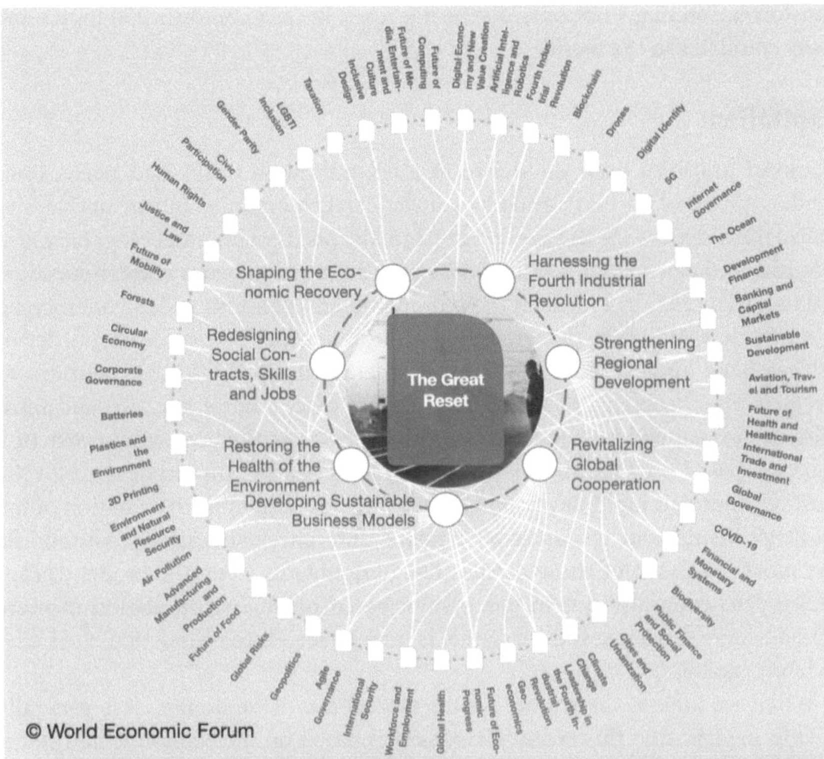

Figure 3.1: Great Reset Transformation Map
Source: https://www.weforum.org/agenda/2020/06/now-is-the-time-for-a-great-reset/

Figure 3.1 is a transformation map that explains the Great Reset with seven main elements and shows the sub-components for each element (World Economic Forum Strategic Intelligence, 2020). According to Figure 3.1, the key elements of the big reset are shaping economic recovery, tapping into the gains of the fourth industrial revolution, strengthening regional development, stimulating global cooperation, developing sustainable business models, restoring nature's health, and redesigning social contracts, skills and occupations. This transformation map, which explains in detail the sub-components that are very interrelated and should be considered under multiple headings, gives an idea about how the big reset, which does not have a roadmap yet will take place. The "Strategic Intelligence Unit" of the World Economic Forum has prepared such transformation maps not only on the big reset, but also on over 250 topics and many countries in the world.

Capitalism

Mankind has lived with the desire to meet unlimited wants and needs since the day it existed on earth and has felt the need to organize in various ways to realize these desires. As the ages progressed, the needs of human beings have also changed, and new techniques and ideas have emerged to better meet these needs and requirements. As a result of these thoughts, an 'economic order' has emerged in the society. Whether this emerging economic order is a successful order or not has been understood by looking at whether it offers effective solutions to the economic problems of the society. In this case, a more effective and most efficient service will be achieved on whichever basis the economic order of a society is based on. Questions such as what kind of a system can be used for the most efficient and rapid development and the most equitable distribution of the country's insufficient resources have raised different economic system models. The most discussed of these models has undoubtedly been the model of capitalism. The capitalist system is a system based on the accumulation of more capital, where this accumulated capital is transformed into production and based on labor capital.

When we look at the studies on the emergence of capitalism, it is generally tried to explain that this economic system is based on the economic and social developments that emerged in Europe since the 11th century, and it is tried to be explained with the internal dynamics of Europe, which has been in constant progress since this century, and the discovery of America. It will be seen that very little place is given to colonialism. It is also frequently observed that agricultural reform is the basis of these internal dynamics (Landes, 1998). The only fact that has not changed since the emergence of capitalism, perhaps will never change, and pushes it to expand like a big bang, is that it is based on an ever-increasing capital accumulation.

It is possible to talk about the four most known and popular definitions of capitalism. The first of these definitions characterizes it simply as "Capitalism". The second definition relates capitalism to the tendency to monopolize economic production. Accordingly, capitalism is an economic mode of production that wants to dominate the market completely and keep it under its control.

The other definition is that of Marx and bases capitalism essentially on the alienating relationship between production and labor. Accordingly, if there are capital owners (bourgeoisie) who have taken the means of production under their control and monopolized it, and workers (proletariat) who offer their physical strength to the employer for a certain wage to be employed in this production, it means that the essence of capitalism has been formed there (Marx, 2015).

The fourth definition is that of Weber and basically relates it to rationality. According to Weber, capitalism is certainly not the drive to make unlimited profits, but rather the restraint of this drive by reason. In short, for Weber, capitalism is a rational economic production system. As a matter of fact, according to him, for capitalism to exist, Rational Capital Accounting, Freedom of Money, Rational Technology, Rational Law, Free Labor must exist, and sixth and lastly, Commercialization of Economic Life must have taken place. Based on these elements, Weber defines capitalism as the rational organization of free workforce. (Weber, 1999).

Stakeholder Capitalism

The world needs a sustainable and collective effort. This effort is shifting from a growth and profitability-oriented approach to a stakeholder-oriented, value production approach. The "stakeholder economy", which is defined as the new economy model, is being adopted by more and more companies with its new opportunities and sustainable-based approach. Moreover, this approach creates significant differences in reputation and marketing processes for companies.

With the emergence of different lines of business and increasing demand, many companies in almost every field whose operations increase are essentially in charge of an economy of their own. The world experienced the best example of how some extraordinary situations can affect and change the way of doing business. Increasing impacts of climate change, loss of natural resources, social unrest based on working conditions and finally the COVID-19 pandemic have also reshaped expectations regarding the roles of companies. To continue to thrive and grow, companies need to place greater emphasis on creating long-term and sustainable value that will embrace all the demands of societies and the planet.

Capitalism has so far embodied either in the form of state capitalism or shareholder capitalism based on Milton Friedman (1971). Schwab (2019) proposes stakeholder capitalism, a type of capitalism that is profit-oriented, pollutes the environment as much as it wants, and focuses only on increasing production, instead of a capitalism that will be beneficial to people, progress and our planet. In stakeholder capitalism, which is the opposite of shareholder capitalism, the goal is to improve the well-being of people and the planet. In this type of capitalism, companies must focus on long-term value generation and environmental, social and governance values (ESGs). This understanding of capitalism was put forward by Schwab and Kroos (1971) in 1971. According to Ulagay (2021), stakeholder capitalism argues that the neoliberal approach, which argues that companies should not have any goals other than profit, is outdated and emerges as a different understanding that benefits all stakeholders of the company.

With more than a year of interviews and research with business leaders, activists, academics, employees in various industries, McKinsey has provided five principal recommendations to companies that want to make stakeholder engagement a reality.

In the first item, the board of directors needs to be included in the process. Because the boards of directors, which are responsible for the long-term interests of the companies, determine and manage the strategy within this framework. In the report, it is emphasized that for stakeholder participation to take place, due to these characteristics of commitment, it must start from the board of directors. To achieve this, two different but complementary approaches are proposed. One of these; the appointment of independent members with a variety of experience, skills and interests to the board who can reflect the concerns and priorities of a wider range of stakeholders, rather than just shareholders (McKinsey'den Paydaş Kapitalizmi Raporu, 2021).

The other approach is; re-determination of corporate governance principles by considering stakeholders rather than shareholders. Although there are successful examples with long-term results, it is not easy for companies to adopt these approaches. McKinsey; As a transitional step, he recommends that boards initiate 'listening sessions' to at least hear from employees and community leaders. McKinsey explains as the second principle that companies with stakeholder value commit to putting the principles into practice by publishing tangible, achievable and measurable targets. It is emphasized that improving environmental performance, which is likened to a marathon, requires education and commitment. Prioritizing environmental sustainability; It also enables companies to make profits by reducing costs such as energy and packaging (McKinsey'den Paydaş Kapitalizmi Raporu, 2021).

The third article of realizing stakeholder capitalism; It also aims to improve the practices of subcontractors and suppliers. Companies are advised to leverage their expertise and economic strength to achieve this. It is emphasized that a company's sense of responsibility must go beyond its operations, not only economically and environmentally, but also in terms of its impact on consumers, contractors and employees. In stakeholder capitalism, companies are invited to create long-term positive effects on consumers with the products and services they offer. The report exemplifies the fourth principle that Swiss food company Nestle has added whole grains and vitamins by reducing the amount of sugar used in breakfast cereals (McKinsey'den Paydaş Kapitalizmi Raporu, 2021).

Believing that employees are a valuable resource and investing in them takes its place as the fifth principle in stakeholder capitalism. Thanks to this principle, companies become more attractive to prospective recruits in the long run. Employee satisfaction, loyalty and productivity increase.

The idea of stakeholder capitalism coupled with the big reset can partially answer the question of how and why this reset should happen. According to the designers of the Great Reset, global leaders, companies, and international institutions are striving in good faith to improve living conditions around the world. It has been proven that the neoliberal economic approach, which has been reaping its fruits in the last 40–50 years, does not give the desired result and is a wrong way. For this reason, it is necessary to abandon the growth model and the 'tyranny of growth' (Schwab & Malleret, 2020) that has been defended until now, and that the state should no longer let the functioning of the market go. A more virtuous capitalism will be possible by involving stakeholders in the plans. The COVID-19 crisis has become a litmus test of who is "swimming naked" while promoting stakeholder capitalism.

Crises in the World

The crisis is often described by social scientists; It is used synonymously with words such as "sudden deterioration", "great distress" and "depression". However, the crisis; is that some previously unknown, unaccounted for or unforeseen developments may have consequences that will seriously affect the state at the macro level, and the firms, and therefore the entrepreneurs, at the micro level. From the point of view of the state, companies, and the public, it is seen that the crisis and inflation are an economic problem. However, in the case of hyperinflation, a crisis is mentioned when the prices of goods and services in the country unexpectedly and suddenly increase at a very high level.

After the effects of the 1929 World Depression, which remained the biggest crisis experienced in the development process of capitalism, no major economic and financial crisis was encountered in the world economy until the late 1960s. In the meantime, it is possible to talk about a financial crisis in England, although it is not very large. In 1956, the troubles of the Suez Canal Company caused a financial crisis for England in the modern sense. Although England had a current account surplus in 1956 and 1957, the sterling remained under pressure due to the negative effects in the country's international trade, and the Bank of England was forced to use almost all of its dollar reserves to maintain the constant value of the sterling against the dollar (Boughton, 2001).

The post-1970 period, which started with the collapse of the Bretton Woods System and gained momentum with the two oil crises, began to be defined by severe crises again. In this period, especially the increasing mobility of financial capital at the international level brought along financial crises with increasing frequency in both developed and developing countries. The debt crisis, which was experienced as a result of the failure of developing countries to fulfill their external debt obligations at the beginning of the 1980s, led to serious economic problems, the effects of which continued for a long time in the developed and developing world, and the contraction of the world economy as a whole.

From the 1980s to the 1990s, Latin American countries made financial reforms to deepen their financial systems and increase the efficiency of investments. These practices for the liberalization of national capital markets, which gained weight with the financial pressure process in Latin America, failed in the 1980s. Giving weight to financial liberalization policies without institutional arrangements by removing financial pressure has made financial markets open to crisis (Williamson & Mahar, 2002).

The crisis that started in Thailand in July 1997 and spread to other Asian countries and then to other countries of the world in a short time, called the Asian crisis, is essentially a financial crisis. The Asian crisis was caused by the policy of raising the interest rates in order to attract the foreign capital back into the country, the high current debt ratios and the weakening of the economy due to the weakness of the financial institutions (Devrim, 2001). The financial crisis, which first started in February 1997 and spread to the regional economies and the world with Thailand's devaluation of its currency Baht on July 2, spread to the Philippines, Malaysia, Indonesia, South Korea, and Hong Kong, and affected these countries, respectively. has taken under. For example, 75 % of companies in Indonesia have gone bankrupt.

The 2008 Economic Crisis or the Great Recession are the economic developments that emerged in the last months of 2008 and adversely affected many countries. Compared to the 1929 World Economic Depression, this crisis became especially visible in September 2008. It is thought that the sudden depreciation of the real estate market in the USA and the resulting increase in personal bankruptcies in held sales triggered this crisis.

Industrial Revolutions

This concept, which is expressed as the first industrial revolution, also known as Industry 1.0, constitutes the first step of the four stages of the industrialization process. While it is stated that the start date of Industry 1.0 dates to the 1650s, it is a process that continued until the 1840s. However, the social worker movements that started in the 1840s interrupted this process in 1840 and 1848. Industry 1.0, which emerged as a product of many historical developments, emerged around a political, economic, and social ground. These favorable conditions have emerged in England (Hobsbawm, 2008)

The first Industrial Revolution took place in England in the mid-18th century and was powered by the invention of the steam engine. In the second half of the 19th century, the Second Industrial Revolution emerged in Europe and the USA. This revolution was characterized by mass production and the replacement of steam with chemical and electrical energy. To meet the increasing demand, various technologies have been developed in industry and mechanization that allow increased productivity, such as the automated assembly line (Pereira & Romero, 2017, p. 1207). In addition to the transformations Industry 1.0 has made in the fields of production and transportation, it is perhaps the transformation in the social field, where the effect is felt the most. The rapid increase in the population of Europe in this period, the fundamentally shocking effect of Industry 1.0 triggered the migration flow from rural to urban areas. Near the end of the 18th century, with the liquidation of feudalism, peasants who did not own land began to migrate to industrial centers in waves (Mahiroğulları, 2005).

The increasing urban population has led to the establishment of new settlements outside the city centers. While these new settlements were called "suburbs", it caused socio-cultural differences between the suburbs and those living in the city centers. This migration movement, which spread over a long period of time, led to the birth of a new class. With this migration movement, which revealed the working class, the workers faced with "unemployment" because of the labor supply exceeding the demand for labor, even if they did not experience difficulties in the industrial centers they came from. In such a situation, the workers, who had to accept the employer's conditions unconditionally, continued to work under difficult and bad conditions until the regulations that prevented the exploitation of labor in labor relations. Workers started to revolt against this difficult situation and the capitalist order identified with the machine.

This period, also known as the second industrial revolution or Industry 2.0, covers the years between 1850 and 1914. England, which played the leading role in the first industrial revolution, left its place to Germany and the United States in the second industrial revolution. The main actors of the industry of this period are electric motor, telephone telegraph, internal combustion engine etc. (Günay, Öcal & Öcalan, 2018). This period also bears the characteristic of being a period in which supply and demand converged tremendously until the economic depression of 1929, despite the technological development in the past.

With the development of technology as of the 1960–1990 period, the third industrial revolution began to emerge. Thus, the production of software that is being used today has started and the process of digitalization of information has come to life. At this point, with the implementation of the new software in question, the use of new production tools and new generation hardware has begun (Özdoğan, 2018).

Emerging new technologies and increasing production capacities in this context have led to the emergence of new markets. In this third stage of globalization, each of the current cost items in production has started to be followed closely by industries. In this context, customers were demanding both low-priced and high-quality products. The only condition for this was to keep costs under control. To control costs, industrial activities are divided into "value-added" and "non-value-added" activities. At this point, a search for an enterprise, which is defined as outsourcing in terms of industrial activities, has been started. The outsourcing of industries provided the opportunity to produce high quality products as well as offering cost advantages. Thus, during the third industrial revolution, the supply chain began to gain a global-scale quality. In this context, no product has started to be produced in just one place anymore. The outsourcing and the fact that, among other functions, production activities were started to be performed by external actors, many of the factories became quieter and more desolate places. This period of industrial stages is also defined as the branding period. In this context, they provided the opportunity to develop brands by increasing their global characteristics and directing almost all their production processes to external sources in order to further develop the brands they produce (Görçün, 2016).

While the fourth industrial revolution solves difficult jobs and tasks with automation and technology, it also brings smart systems, also called cyber-physical systems, that can change people to the agenda. It can be said that the digital transformation, which became public with the discourse of "Industry 4.0" in 2011, brought both new business models and the need for a workforce with different competencies to the agenda. In addition, the emergence of the smart society formed within the framework of this transformation shows that a new organization and life codes are knitted with new social and global power networks based on the technology revolution.

It can be stated that the radical changes that started to emerge because of the blending of industrial opportunities with technology, which makes the fourth industrial revolution different from other industrial revolutions, are based on more innovative and efficiency bases compared to the inventions and inventions that emerged at the turning points of the first, second and partially third industrial revolutions. Therefore, the need for new solutions at every stage and in every dimension of this innovative structure also reveals new modelling requirements. The fourth industrial revolution is a way of describing the series of both ongoing and impending transformations in systems that have encompassed and become commonplace for almost everyone. As a matter of fact, this revolution is as new a stage in human development as the first, second and third industrial revolutions, and is powered by the increasing accessibility and interaction of a number of extraordinary technologies (Schwab, 2019).

The Great Reset and the 4th Industrial Revolution

One of the main components of the Great Reset is to take advantage of the possibilities of Industry 4.0. Klaus Schwab (2017) wrote a book on the Fourth Industrial Revolution in 2017, the Great Reset in 2020, and subsequently on Stakeholder capitalism, and presented these topics in a way that complements each other. The Covid-19 environment has given legitimacy to the constant monitoring of people for vital reasons, and this is the case in authoritarian regimes like China. It was instantly accepted and praised and supported by global elites.

With Industry 4.0, it is planned that products and machines will communicate with each other and with people. In addition, systems will be able to make decisions on their own in many matters, thanks to the artificial intelligence they will have. With this design, what is planned in the first place is to minimize errors in many areas of life, especially in production, and to achieve more efficient processes by using resources effectively. In addition, it will be possible to reflect the individual demands of people to production instantly with Industry 4.0. The digital transformation that will occur in the production processes will bring economic, individual, social, national and global changes, especially the functioning of the companies. Schwab (2017) cites physical, digital and biological megatrends as the driving force of these changes. Listing the positive and negative aspects of the changes, Schwab does not provide information on what to do to avoid negative effects. This study, which is loaded with information, does not offer a clear view on how the elites and policymakers, who hold a large part of the world economy, should follow.

Industry 4.0 is examined under two separate sub-titles, Benefiting from the 4th Industrial Revolution and Redefining Social Contracts, Skills, and Occupations within the scope of the Big Reset. With the radical changes to be experienced with digital transformation, some professions will disappear, and many new professions will emerge. As existing skills lose their function and many new skills are needed, there will be a need to redefine the employee-employer relationship. Industry 4.0 will be one of the main actors in the change of many basic elements in our lives and in the design of life in the new era called the Great Reset. One of the current debates is how to prevent the negative effects of individuals, societies, and nations, which are increasingly condemned to the hands of artificial intelligence, by means of developing technology and products with this technology.

Conclusion

COVID- Although the 19 lockdowns are progressively relaxing, concern about the world's social and economic outlook is growing. There is reason to be concerned: a severe economic slump has already begun, and we may be on the verge of the greatest depression since the 1930s. While this is a foreseeable conclusion, it is not unavoidable.

To achieve a better outcome, the world must act collectively and swiftly to renew all aspects of our societies and economies, from education to social contracts and working conditions. Every country, from the United States to China, must participate, and every industry, from oil and gas to technology, must be transformed. In short, we need a "Great Reset" of capitalism.

There are many reasons to pursue a Great Reset, but COVID-19 is the most pressing. The pandemic has already claimed the lives of hundreds of thousands of people, making it one of the deadliest public-health crises in recent memory. And it's far from over, with casualties still piling up in many corners of the globe. Economic development, public debt, employment, and human well-being will all suffer because of this. All of this will exacerbate the already-existing climate and social concerns. The COVID-19 has already been used by several countries to undermine environmental regulations and enforcement.

Together with COVID-19, crises will worsen, making the globe less sustainable, less egalitarian, and more vulnerable. To avoid this scenario, incremental measures and ad hoc solutions will not sufficient. Our economic and social structures must be rebuilt from the ground up. Similarly, people have shown a strong readiness to accept sacrifices for healthcare and other critical professions, as well as vulnerable groups like the elderly. In a shift toward the kind of stakeholder capitalism to which they had previously given lip service, many corporations have stepped up to support their workers, customers, and local communities.

The Great Reset's agenda would be broken into three parts. The first would lead to more egalitarian outcomes in the market. To attain this purpose, governments should improve coordination (for example, in tax, regulatory, and fiscal policy), upgrade trade agreements, and create conditions for a "stakeholder economy." In the face of decreasing revenue bases and mounting public debt, governments have a strong incentive to seek such action. The second component of the Great Reset agenda would ensure that investments achieve common values such as equality and sustainability. Large-scale spending projects, which several are pursuing, offer a substantial opportunity for progress in this area.

The third and final goal of a Great Reset agenda is to exploit discoveries from the Fourth Industrial Revolution to promote the public good, notably through addressing health and social challenges. Businesses, universities, and others teamed together in the aftermath of the COVID-19 outbreak to investigate diagnostics, treatments, and possibly immunizations; create testing centers; devise infection-tracing systems; and provide telemedicine. Consider what could be accomplished if everyone put out similar coordinated efforts. progress in this field.

The COVID-19 disaster is wreaking havoc on people's lives in every part of the planet. Its only legacy, though, does not have to be tragedy. The pandemic, on the other hand, represents a once-in-a-lifetime opportunity to ponder, reimagine, and reset our civilization in order to achieve a healthier, more equal, and prosperous future.

In the Covid-19 process, the minimum state principle of neoclassical economics has left its place to a state that intervenes more in the markets, and this state has turned into a smart and controlling state with digitalization. Since the Great Reset was planned along with digital transformation, there is a very strong possibility that states will eventually turn into a technocratic state. On the other hand, taking steps back from globalization with the 2008 crisis and trade wars pushed the countries in the world to regionalization. With the closure of the borders during the pandemic process, disruptions have been experienced in the supply chains and this has strengthened the regionalization flows. It seems unlikely that these trends will reverse now, so global leaders are making an effort to protect global trade and capital flows from harm.

The Covid-19 epidemic and its aftermath brought to light the main points that institutional economists criticize the market economy, and in this process, the inadequacies in economic life could not be dealt with without government intervention. The already corrupt income distribution has become even more unequal and the reforms that need to be made to ensure the justice of income distribution in societies have started to give an emergency signal. The teachings of institutional economics, which contributed to the mainstream economy by incorporating concepts such as the environment, unions, improvement of working conditions, contracts, and transaction costs into economic analysis, came to the fore again in this crisis period.

When the writings and meetings about the Great Reset are examined, it is seen that the discussions are currently focused on the subject of "why" and tend to legitimize this idea, but the "how" of this reset has not yet been discussed. For example, there is no roadmap on how to solve problems such as income inequalities, hunger, poverty, environmental pollution, and financial problems produced by the capitalist global system. It seems that the global elites, big companies, and policy makers – mostly in the field of technology – are making a new plan and design by looking at Covid-19 on the bright side and saying, "let this be a lesson to us".

İpek Senem Gedikoğlu

Chapter 4 Gender Inequality and She-Cession

Introduction

Joseph Alois Schumpeter suggests that capitalism is not sustainable. Its institutions will erode from within and lead to self-destruction by opening the gates to socialism in parallel with Kuhn's paradigm shift.

As an economist, Schumpeter explains the source of lasting capitalism with revolutions and rejuvenation of the economy via the new production methods, products, new transformation roads, markets and organization methods (Schumpeter, 2007), which author describes the process with the "*creative destruction*". As in any financial trend, a paradigm shift in the spotlight of Covid-19 has opened to discussion. The question is: will it break? This is what we will be focusing on in this chapter by taking women employees' and women's' rights under focus.

World Economic Situation and Prospects 2020 report of UN calls the pandemic: "*The Great Disruption*" (United Nations, 2021). The report indicates that the long-run economic repercussions of the pandemic would have been even harsher if it would not be the government interventions, both fiscal and monetary. However, it has turned the crisis into a trade-off between health and economics. This trade-off is even grimmer for countries with high debt rates (United Nations, 2021a).

2021 report illustrates that full recovery for some countries can take a decade since the crisis turned volatile economies further critical. Countries like the U.S.A. and China has almost recovered, but it might take up to two years to entirely recover for the rest (United Nations, 2021b).

Research conducted by DİSK (Devrimci İşçi Sendikaları Konfederasyonu) presents that pandemic caused redundancy rates for women and men are 15.5 % and 12.4 %. Globally 255 million workers were laid off. A narrowly defined rate including the seasonal adjustments is 13.2 % in Turkey, which corresponds to roughly 3.6 million workers. It is above the 8.8 % average rate for the world (DİSK-AR, 2021a). Nevertheless, broadly defined unemployment has reached 8.4 million, counting the latest redundancies due to the lift of limitations on dismissing employees in June 2021 and job hunting of discouraged workers after the termination of pandemic restrictions in July 2021 (DİSK-AR, 2021b).

However, women and girls are the worst affected by the disruption. Gender equality has taken a big step back, 40 years to be precise (UNCTAD, 2021). Most women had to leave their jobs to help their families. Gender inequality has further strengthened with education disruptions, unwanted pregnancies and violence towards women and girls (United Nations, 2021b).

Primarily, 70 % of worldwide health professionals and 90 % of caregivers in OECD countries are a woman. They have a vital role in fighting against the Covid-19. Thus, more women have been infected by the virus than men. Furthermore, the inaccessibility of regular reproductive health services led to maternal and baby deaths (United Nations, 2021; Chmielewska et al., 2021). Women's' reproductive rights are damaged due to the shortage of medical services and unreachability to family planning. Consequently, 1.4 million undesired babies were born in 2020. However, the worst is another consequence of the pandemic. It's called "*The Shadow Pandemic*": the increase in violence and harassment towards women (United Nations, 2021).

Purple Roof Women's Shelter Foundation's report also confirms the UN report that shelter services and rights have been in practice mostly inaccessible (Mor Çatı, 2021). Moreover, pandemic infused interruption of education as in the Ebola crisis automatically generated negative assumptions on the number of woman students resuming school (United Nations, 2021).

Women in Work Index 2021 report of PwC presents the concerns on the reverse movement towards gender inequality. The existing parity in wages and opportunities has worsened. Negative impacts of Covid-19 regarding the imbalance on woman workers took them back to 2017 regarding inequality.

The prevalent damage of the crisis was on women. Their unemployment rate has reached new highs because 40 % of women work in the distressed sectors. Hence, women's labor participation rate has decreased 3.3 %, leading to a higher unemployment rate, approximately 15 % for the 26 % of the entire woman labor market (Day & Çilingir, 2021).

However, the disruption had other overwhelming effects for women with young children. With the schools closed down, women had to stay at home for childcare. She-cession is the phenomenon that unemployment of women increases in times of recession. These rates were even higher for women of color in the US (Warrell, 2021).

Gender In The Workplace

Gender has always been a factor of discrimination in the labor force. Vertical segregation, which includes the glass ceiling, glass escalator, the labyrinth,

Table 4.1: Some of women's workplace issues

Some Examples of Gender Inequality in the Workplace			
Gender bias in hiring	Gender discrimination	Vertical Segregation	Glass ceiling
Glass escalator	The labrinth	Horizontal segregation	Gender wage gap
Informal economy	Worker exploitation	Social security	Job security
Work-family balance	Paid maternity-leave	Child-care	Second shift
Single parenthood	Paid sick-leave	Job gender traits	Gender communication
Questioned authority	Unequal opportunities	Workplace harassment	Concrete wall

horizontal discrimination, gender wage gap, work-family balance (WFB) is merely some of these issues that a woman confronts day to day basis.

Gender has always been an issue in the labor market from the "*concrete wall*" to the 70s global movement of women in the labor market. The glass ceiling, which prevents women from climbing the corporate ladder, has gradually been eradicated and lead to the "*labyrinth*" (p. 6). It describes the intricate path to success that only some can manage (Eagly & Carli, 2007). Depending on the sector and position, some of these issues and day to day experiences are listed in Table 4.1.

However, these topics get harsher in a recession due to birth and childcare attributes. Hence, they are the earliest to get redundant. The assumption underneath is that the primary priority for women is children instead of the paid work. Therefore, they cannot be as productive as men, although they are frequently paid less for the same job.

Some of these struggles are clear, while others can be more covert. After a lifetime of exposure and internalization, most women tend to normalize them. An example can be that in horizontal segregation, most women work in marketing and communication-related departments and positions, resulting from the conditioning as a part of their socialization process since childhood.

Durkheim describes this as an extension of the division of labor to create the modern lifestyle (Lukes, 2013). It assigns genders to discrepant work and house realms. Thus, employees are in cohesion with the gender of the employee. Hence,

Table 4.2: Feminene and masculine traits

Feminene Traits	Masculine Traits
Friendly	Authoritative
Timid	Athletic
Creative	Aggresive
Obedient	Domineering
Affectionate	Competitive
Talkative	Self-confident
Sympathetic	Ambitious

women are amalgamated with emotional labor (Wharton, 2012). In which communication plays the dominating role as a feminine trait.

Hofstede (2001) states that culture is the coding of the mind, and in a way, gender, race, class, religion are all parts of the process. Table 4.2 below, illustrates the assigned traits to the two main genders (Lupetow et al., 1995; cited by Caterall & Maclaren, 2002).

Sex and gender refer to two different meanings. Sex might be biologically assigned to a person, while gender corresponds to a more socialization aspect of the sex (Unger, 1979; cited by Brannon, 2011).

In this period, social life was re-shaped based on work by creating a division of labor within the household. Before the industrial revolution, both genders were working and even fighting together. Division of labor caused manual factory work to be associated with men (Lukes, 2013; Brannon, 2011).

These roles and traits consciously or unintentionally design and dictate every day of men and women in any social surrounding. However, molding persons into hypothetical figures and figurines favor comfort over competency.

Work has been built for men based on masculine qualities via reinforcements. Therefore, women raised with these characteristics are more successful at managerial positions (Billing, 2011). However, some sectors and positions like assistantship, nurses, teachers, etc., require care, emotional intelligence and communication. Thus, they are automatically associated with women. Conversely, feminine characteristics dominating sectors have another phenomenon, *the glass escalator*. In which men are automatically linked with the leadership position, regardless of women running it.

On the other hand, sectors like finance, engineering, technology are founded on masculine characteristics. Often, they hire men over women and recruitment might mean a wage gap. Therefore, entering a job is an issue but keeping it is an entirely different story. To exemplify, Sarah Cooper was working in the IT sector. After her resignation, she wrote about her problematic experiences (See Cooper, 2018).

It is witnessed that working from home has led to more work to family and family to work conflicts. There were a time smartphone was interrupting the personal time of workers. It has reached a new peak with the pandemic since everything is online. The balance is no longer there, but data are still restricted since the health crisis continues. Later, in the childcare section, "*the second shift*" will be elaborated.

Labor Force and She-Cession

Pandemic has touched the entire labor force, pushed workers home. Redundancy, work from home (WFH), childcare, WFB become the main issues for this period. However, it affected women more firmly than men, unlike any recession. Restrictions primarily disturbed the service sector, which mainly recruits women. The discrepancy from the fiscal recession is the principal impact on finance and construction.

Furthermore, the closure of the schools and daycares increased the burden of childcare (Alon et al., 2020). However, it is assumed to be temporary due to the governmental encouragement plans and the role of fathers. This prediction might be for the developed countries (Alon et al., 2020).

Women had to quit their jobs for care, which deepened the effects of the Covid-19 and specifically on single mothers (Nagaraj, 2021; Alon et al., 2020). Usual support systems like grandparents, neighbors and friends, has become unavailable due to social restrictions (Alon et al., 2020). UN Women report highlights that until August 2020, redundancy rates lead 50 million women to pass the poverty line. As UN Women and UNCTAD state that the effects of the pandemic are gender biased. It has increased inequality (UN Women, 2020a; UN Women, 2020b; Zarrilli & Luomaranta, 2021).

Data from the Turkish Statistic Institution (TUIK) between 2014 and 2020 presents that the labor force has shrunk. The participation rate has also gone through a similar downward movement for all sexes. Nonetheless, the low participation rate of women (30 %) is chronic to Turkey. However, this data does not cover the informal workers.

Table 4.3: Eurostat labour participation and unemployment rates for women in the Europe

	Labour Participation Rate		Unemployment Rate	
	2019	**2020**	**2019**	**2020**
European Union – 27 countries	**63**	**62,5**	**7,1**	**7,4**
Euro area – 19 countries	63	62,3	7,9	8,2
Belgium	61,7	61	4,9	5,4
Bulgaria	66	64,3	3,9	4,8
Czechia	68,1	67,1	2,4	3
Denmark	72	71,4	5,3	6
Germany	72,8	73,2	2,7	3,4
Estonia	71,9	71	4,8	6,6
Ireland	64,2	62,4	4,7	5,7
Greece	47,3	47,5	21,5	19,8
Spain	57,9	55,7	16	17,4
France	62,5	62,2	8,4	8
Croatia	57,1	56,9	7,2	7,6
Italy	50,1	49	11,1	10,2
Cyprus	65,2	64,3	8	7,6
Latvia	70,7	70,2	5,4	7,1
Lithuania	72,5	71	5,5	7,7
Luxembourg	63,6	63,9	5,5	7
Hungary	63	62,3	3,5	4,5
Malta	62,8	64,6	4	4,5
Netherlands	74,1	73,9	3,4	4
Austria	69,2	68,3	4,4	5,2
Poland	61,1	61,5	3,6	3,3
Portugal	67,6	66,6	7,2	7,1
Romania	56,8	56,5	3,4	4,7
Slovenia	68,6	67,8	5	5,6
Slovakia	62,4	61,7	6	7,1
Finland	71,8	70,7	6,2	7,5
Sweden	75,4	73,5	7	8,3
Iceland	**81,9**	**77,8**	**3,1**	**5,3**
Norway	73,1	72,7	3,4	4,1
Switzerland	76,3	75,9	4,7	5
Montenegro	49,7	44,4	15,7	18,4
North Macedonia	44,7	45,3	18,4	15,9
Serbia	54,3	54,8	11,2	9,5
Turkey	**32,2**	**29,7**	**16,5**	**14,9**

European Commission shares that they use the nationally collected datasets (European Commission, n.d.). The total participation rate is lower than in 2011. Men's' rate is less than in 2006, while the female rate being lower than in 2015.

However, unemployment is higher for women in Turkey. Though high-school or university education does not make much difference for men, it does for women. Higher education creates less unemployment risk, yet still higher than for men. Therefore, access to education is crucial, particularly during the pandemic. However, this might be because fewer women with a higher education degree are searching for a job.

To summarize, Turkish women have low participation and high unemployment rates. Nonetheless, in 2020 participation rate has diminished for all education levels. Consequently, unemployment has decreased for all degrees. Furthermore, quarterly data present that women unemployment rate is above the total and the men for the last two quarters. The annual participation rate is lower than the quarterly figures, especially considering the discouraged workers. Men gradually felt the crisis later when it hit the manufacturing and trade sectors. Pandemic has undermined the gender equality movement to improve this employment gap.

This disruption has created discouraged workers. These employees are not counted in the unemployment but reflected at the participation rates. Moreover, UNCTAD emphasizes the significance of encouraging policies for recovery. They also suggest gender-separated statistics to observe the effects on the women (Zarrilli & Luomaranta, 2021).

Informal Economy and Women

In accord with the service sector, often women are employed in informal economies. Naturally, their employment records are kept unofficial. Therefore, employees working in this sector, for instance, cleaning service providers, babysitters, cooks, usually have no access to social security. The majority of informal sector jobs constitute domestic, home-based workers, street vendors, waste pickers. Of which the first two can be found in urban life (International Labor Organization, 2013).

Table 4.4: Turkish workforce by gender 2014–2020

	Total			Men			Women		
Year	Population over age 15 (million)	Labour Force	Participation rate	Population over age 15 (million)	Labour Force	Participation rate	Population over age 15 (million)	Labour Force	Participation rate
2014	56 986	28 786	50,5	28 145	20 057	71,3	28 841	8 729	30,3
2015	57 854	29 678	51,3	28 573	20 453	71,6	29 281	9 225	31,5
2016	58 720	30 535	52	29 031	20 899	72	29 689	9 637	32,5
2017	59 893	31 643	52,8	29 649	21 484	72,5	30 244	10 159	33,6
2018	60 654	32 274	53,2	30 007	21 801	72,7	30 647	10 473	34,2
2019	61 469	32 549	53	30 372	21 863	72	31 097	10 686	34,4
2020	62 579	30 873	49,3	30 956	21 105	68,2	31 623	9 768	30,9

Table 4.5: Eurostat labour participation rate for Turkey 2006–2020

Labour Participation Rate			
Years	**Total**	**Male**	**Female**
2006	44,6	66,9	22,7
2007	44,6	66,8	22,8
2008	44,9	66,6	23,5
2009	44,3	64,5	24,2
2010	46,3	66,7	26,2
2011	48,4	69,2	27,8
2012	48,9	69,2	28,7
2013	49,5	69,5	29,6
2014	49,5	69,5	29,5
2015	50,2	69,8	**30,4**
2016	50,6	70	31,2
2017	51,5	70,7	32,2
2018	52	70,9	32,9
2019	50,3	68,3	32,2
2020	**47,5**	**65,2**	**29,7**

Table 4.6: Unemployment rate from TUIK between the ages 15–64

Unemployment Rate				
	Percentage		**Thousands**	
Year	**Men**	**Women**	**Men**	**Women**
2014	9,2	12,2	1800	1039
2015	9,4	12,9	1874	1165
2016	9,8	14	1988	1323
2017	9,6	14,4	2008	1429
2018	9,7	14,2	2061	1452
2019	12,7	16,8	2684	1758
2020	12,6	15,3	2580	1460

In total, 260 million workers work from home, manufacturing, textile workers, self-employed and teleworkers are a few examples from the developed and emerging countries. Meanwhile, self-employment, industrial workers and chipping in family members are the types seen in developing countries.

Table 4.7: Unemployment rate from TUIK including gender and education

Unemployment Rate								
	Total		**High School**		**Vocational High School**		**Higher Education**	
Year	**Men**	**Women**	**Men**	**Women**	**Men**	**Women**	**Men**	**Women**
2014	9,2	12,2	9,3	19	8	19,3	7,7	15,5
2015	9,4	12,9	9,5	20,3	7,7	18,1	7,6	16,3
2016	9,8	14	10,5	21,1	8,7	20,6	8,8	16,9
2017	9,6	14,4	10,2	21,3	9	20,6	8,7	18,4
2018	9,7	14,2	10,3	20,2	8,2	20,8	9,1	17,1
2019	12,7	16,8	13,3	22,9	11,6	25,8	10,3	18,5
2020	12,6	15,3	13,7	20,3	11,6	23,5	10,1	16,8

Table 4.8: Unemployment and participation rates from TUIK for women and education level

	Womens' Labour Participation Rate		**Womens' Unemployment Rate**	
	2020	**2019**	**2020**	**2019**
Illiterate	19	23,1	6,8	6,8
Literate	22	25,8	11,7	13
Primary school	29,8	33,8	8,7	10,6
Middle school	28,3	33,9	18,3	20,3
Vocational middle school	21,1	24,3	18	19,3
High school	30,8	35	20,3	22,9
Vocational high school	38,5	43,7	23,5	25,8
Higher education	67,4	73,1	16,8	18,5

Eighty-six percentage of 260 million are in developing and emerging countries. Eighty-four percentage of it takes place in all sectors but agriculture. Majorly this economy is active in East and South-Eastern Asia (36 %) and Southern Asia (26 %). Moreover, 146.8 million of 260 are women and 129.4 million are in the developing and emerging economies. Nevertheless, the number of home-based women employees are higher in Sub-Saharan Africa (66 %), Latin America and the Caribbean (67 %) and the Middle East and North Africa (68 %) regions (Bonnet et al., 2021).

Table 4.9: Employment rate and population in thousands in the Turkish informal sector

			Men			Women		
Year	**Total**	**Informal Total**	**Total**	**Informal**	**Rate of change**	**Total**	**Informal**	**Rate of change**
2019	32549	9896	21863	6010.6	0.27	10686	3885.4	0.36
2020	30872	8426.2	21105	5219.3	0.24	9768	3206.9	0.32

WIEGO highlights that home-based employees without access to information and communication technologies are having a hard time adjusting to the pandemic. Consequently, home-based employees of these nations are severely affected by the crisis (Bonnet et al., 2021). Within this categorization, Turkey is considered an emerging economy rather than a developing one. However, a 2014 UN report sorted Turkey under the developing economies headline.

In Turkey, the informal economy is sizeable as in other developing countries. However, its labor force shrunk with the pandemic, as in Table 4.9. Women's involvement with the sector is higher than men. Almost one-third of employed women work irregularly. Therefore, the impact of the disruption has been felt more harshly. Their employment rate has decreased by 4 %.

An intense drop in the employment rate is also visible in this economy. Conversely, there has been a steady increase in the services sector for women since the early 2000s. Signs of the pandemic are evident in the number of employed persons. The decline in non-agricultural sectors might be rising from the increasing unemployment rates for women. Explicitly a 4 % drop might explain it.

Most women in the world works informally without social security, insurance, a retirement plan, a union, collective bargaining rights, work security or concisely without any worker rights. In total, there are 2 billion employees, of which 740 million are women. Hence, approximately 20 % of women work in the informal sector (ILO, 2018). Significantly they are raising the next generations within these skimmed and unstable work conditions.

Childcare and the Second Shift

Household chores and childcare, which are traditionally regarded as the responsibility of women, is called the second shift. However, this custom is changing over time. Usually, it was automatically expected of women after their full-time paid work. Therefore, it is called "unpaid work", which is regularly taken

Table 4.10: ILO: Turkish employment rate in the informal economy

Employment in the Informal Economy (thousands)				
	All Sectors		**Broad Service Sector**	
Years	**Male**	**Female**	**Male**	**Female**
2004	6572.4	3443.4	2426	518.9
2005	7950.7	3376.1	3440.4	634
2006	7814.5	3379.9	3437.8	694.1
2007	7610	3307.1	3366.5	665.9
2008	7323.3	3327.6	3146.8	667.1
2009	6036.2	3551.7	2383.4	733.8
2010	6142.5	3888.8	2311.5	749.3
2011	6241.6	4174.2	2238.4	831.8
2012	5863.9	4103.6	2003.5	872.8
2013	5543.1	4106.9	1854.9	901
2014	5508.9	3903.5	1918.5	979.5
2015	5369.2	3890.3	1870	1026.4
2016	5549.2	3847.7	1980.4	1084.5
2017	5804.9	4061.6	2094.3	1195.6
2018	5932	4054.5	2197.9	1304.5
2019	6010.6	3885.4	2361.1	1310.5
2020	**5219.3**	**3206,9**	**1872.8**	**1036.2**

Table 4.11: TUIK informal economy employment rate

Informal Economy Employment by Sectors and Sex (percentage)						
	Agriculture			**Non-agriculture**		
Year	**Male**	**Female**	**Total**	**Male**	**Female**	**Total**
2014	71,8	**94,4**	**82,3**	21,1	**25,9**	**22,3**
2015	70,2	94	81,2	20,2	24,1	21,2
2016	72,2	94,3	82,1	20,8	24,2	21,7
2017	74,4	94,2	83,3	21	24,9	22,1
2018	76,2	90,9	82,7	21,2	24,9	22,3
2019	79,5	95,7	86,6	22,4	24,2	23
2020	76,2	**94,3**	**83,5**	18,9	**20,2**	**19,3**

for granted. However, the pandemic has increased this burden since lockdown meant more domestic work, childcare, etc.

OECD's average time spared on unpaid work per day for men is 136,5 and for women, it is double: 263,4 minutes. Alternatively, the time spent at work for men and women is 317,8 and 217,7. Finally, the total time spent with paid and unpaid work is 454,3 and 481,1 minutes for men and women. Although the official work hours were added, which is higher for men in the last quarter of 2020, the total workload of women is still greater than men's'. It highlights the role and value of unpaid work.

For Turkey, unpaid work is 67,6 and 305 minutes for men and women. Conversely, paid work is 358,3 and 133,9 (second lowest among OECD countries after Italy) and in total 425,8 and 439 respectively. However, unpaid work is also work (OECD, 2021).

The reason for women's' employment was the economic downturn, which required more income to the household and its attainability was dependent on two working partners. What has changed with the second shift in the early 21st century? Women started to request men to take responsibility, to equally share the household (Hochschild & Machung, 2003).

However, requesting help was not easy, depending on the couple's power dynamics, personal values regarding roles and relationship type. However, spouses seldom were enthusiastic about the additional workload. Thus, they presented avoidance, substitution and even used patriarchal arguments. Only the egalitarian men immediately accepted the extra work (Hochschild & Machung, 2003).

Furthermore, there is an emotional expense in dealings with children because of the imbalanced household role division. Men do not know about their children's needs and want, and women are like commanders carrying all the responsibility without having quality time with them. Therefore, balanced roles and responsibilities within a household create healthy families and generations (Hochschild & Machung, 2003).

Conversely, within time trends in household chores have changed for men. There have been fluctuations. They did more chores for a while, then suddenly stopped it around the mid-90s. Covid-19 created such a downward trend, but its permanence relies on the length of this health crisis.

More inclusive policymaking is required to equalize the gender difference, focusing on the maternal and paternal leaves, childcare services within the firms. It was already hard to see childcare services in the pre-pandemic for-profit organizations, but now it appears utterly improbable (Hochschild & Machung, 2003).

Table 4.12: Paid maternity leave in OECD countries

Paid Maternity leave				
	2015	**2016**	**2017**	**2018**
Australia	18	18	18	18
Austria	60	60	60	60
Belgium	32,3	32,3	32,3	32,3
Canada	52	52	51	51
Chile	30	30	30	..
Costa Rica	..	17,3	17,3	..
Czech Republic	110	110	110	63,3
Denmark	50	50	50	50
Estonia	166	166	166	166
Finland	161	161	161	161
France	42	42	42	42
Germany	58	58	58	58
Greece	43	43	43	43
Hungary	160	160	160	160
Iceland	26	26	26	26
Ireland	26	26	26	26
Israel	14	14	15	15
Italy	47,7	47,7	47,7	47,7
Japan	58	58	58	58
Korea	64,9	64,9	64,9	64,9
Latvia	..	94	94	94
Lithuania	..	62	62	62
Luxembourg	42	42	33,3	37,3
Mexico	12	12	12	12
Netherlands	16	16	16	16
New Zealand	16	18	18	18
Norway	91	91	91	91
Poland	52	52	52	52
Portugal	30,1	30,1	30,1	30,1
Slovak Republic	164	164	164	164
Slovenia	52,1	52,1	52,1	52,1
Spain	16	16	16	16
Sweden	60	55,7	55,7	55,7
Switzerland	14	14	14	14
Turkey	16	16	16	16
United Kingdom	39	39	39	39

Table 4.12: Continued

Paid Maternity leave				
United States	0	0	0	0
OECD Average	**54,1**	**54**	**53,8**	**53,2**

The table above illustrates the paid maternity leave according to the countries within years until 2018. It gives an idea of the circumstances of women workers with children in the pre-pandemic world. Peculiarly, the OECD average has slightly decreased over the years, which pre-Covid descending trend is bad news for the women workers and rights. Finally, the highest-paid maternity leave is in Estonia, the Slovak Republic and Finland. Opposingly, the USA does not have any paid maternity leave.

Gender Wage Gap

Many claims and arguments oppose the existence of the gender wage gap. However, gender bias exists for both genders (Wharton, 2012). Yale University experimented on the hiring bias. They send two almost the same cv's to be evaluated by researchers. The result is that 127 researchers decided in favor of the man over the woman candidate. They offered him an extra 4,000 dollar pay (YaleNews, 2012).

The highest levels of women's participation in the labor force are in Iceland, Sweden and New Zealand (Day & Çilingir, 2021). However, it is predictable considering the population size of these countries. Iceland's population is 366,425 (The World Bank, 2021), while Sweden's is around 10 million (The World Bank, 2021) and New Zealand a little over 5 million (Stats NZ, 2021). The gender wage gap may be less in small-sized populations due to the need for the labor force. Consequently, in these nations grander number of women fill upper ranks (Wharton, 2012).

The latest unadjusted and industry-focused table presents the gap for EU27. It was 14.1 in 2019 (Eurostat, 2021). Within EU 27 the highest gap can be observed for Estonia (21.7 %), Germany (19.2 %) and Czechia (18.9 %) and the lowest for Luxembourg (1.3 %) (Eurostat, 2021).

From 35 countries, only the ones above have disclosed their wage gap for 2018 and 2019. It illustrates that for certain lands more than 20 % gap is chronic. Whereas negative gaps emerge in only two, Belgium and Italy.

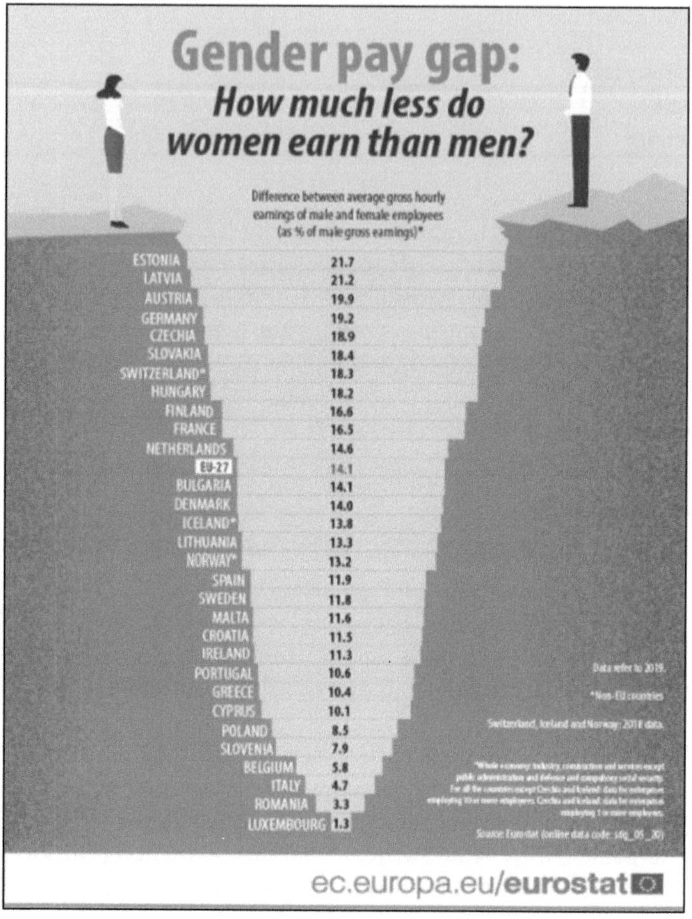

Figure 4.1: Gender Wage Gap (Eurostat, 2021)

Conversely, in 2019 OECD average was 12.5 and the average gap for EU27 was 11.2. Within which Turkey performs lower than the average (10.0) in 2018. Korea is the highest with 31.5 %, which are pursued by Japan (22.5), United States (17.7) and Canada (16.1), United Kingdom (12.3) in 2020 (OECD, 2021).

Moreover, TUIK and ILO joint report suggests that the gap in 2018 is 21.1 %, which is higher for women with lower education levels, 38.6 % (primary school or lower), and for women working in the informal sector, 24.2 % (ILO, 2020).

Table 4.13: Eurostat gender wage gap for countries shared their data for 2018–2019

Gender Wage Gap		
	2018	**2019**
Belgium	-0,3	-0,2
Bulgaria	14,4	14,5
Denmark	17,1	15,8
Germany	17,2	16,2
Spain	6,5	6,5
Croatia	11,1	11,2
Italy	-0,7	-1,6
Latvia	22,2	24,1
Lithuania	15,7	14
Hungary	14,1	18,4
Malta	13,0	11,9
Netherlands	10,2	11,7
Poland	8,6	8,6
Portugal	8,1	9,9
Romania	2,1	2,2
Slovakia	19,5	18,1
Finland	16,4	16,1
Sweden	10,1	9,4

Regardless, inequality in pay rate might be associated with the position rather than the equal pay for equal work (Eurostat, 2017). However, strikes in Dagenham and Iceland in the 1970s has made wage disparity illegal. However, Icelandic women employees' strike for equal pay for equal work in 2018 paints a different picture.

Conversely, in 2010 and 2014 Turkish Statistical Institution has calculated the gender wage gap sorted based on sectors and ranks within organizations. It might have been possible because organizations have to declare wages to the Social Security Institution. Firms cover the insurance of the employees. Therefore, wage differences, in theory, is easier to track. The salaries are based on Turkish Lira (TL). Missing values corresponds to the categories that were not calculated for that year. However, there are researchers like Duman (2020) who are more optimistic about the wage gap.

The pay gap for women is the worst for health professionals; women are almost paid in half. It is observable that in the traditionally masculine traits assuming

Table 4.14: TUIK gender wage gap in 2010 and 2014

Gender Wage Gap							
		Monthly Pay		**Yearly Pay**		**The Difference**	
Position	**Year**	**Men**	**Women**	**Men**	**Women**	**Monthly**	**Yearly**
Manager	2010	3653	3891	48198	52242	-238	-4044
	2014	6643	6138	87670	83893	505	3777
Chief Executives, Senior Officials And Legislators	2010	5477	4481	71773	58197	996	13576
	2014	9406	7675	130618	115600	1731	15018
Administrative And Commercial Managers	2010	3497	4003	46636	54028	-506	-7392
	2014	6507	6593	84913	89107	-86	-4194
Production And Specialised Services Managers	2010	3571	4214	47225	57356	-643	-10131
	2014	6682	6035	85498	77686	647	7812
Hospitality, Retail And Other Services Managers	2010	2222	2143	27940	27938	79	2
	2014	3739	3901	48417	55300	-162	-6883
Professionals	2010	2941	2371	37557	29647	570	7910
	2014	4995	3973	63573	50772	1022	12801
Science And Engineering Professionals	2010	2917	2225	37277	28470	692	8807
	2014	4866	3830	62019	48397	1036	13622
Health Professionals	2010	5033	2578	59805	30379	2455	29426
	2014	6894	4414	89590	57448	2480	32142
Teaching Professionals	2010	2084	2103	24989	25215	-19	-226
	2014	4245	3349	50050	40933	896	9117
Business And Administration Professionals	2010	2879	2535	39609	33893	344	5716
	2014	4659	3991	62447	52492	668	9955
Information And Communications Technology Professionals	2010	3747	3236	47499	43143	511	4356
	2014	6148	6056	77905	78574	92	-669
Legal, Social And Cultural Professionals	2010	2539	2794	33828	35589	-255	-1761
	2014	4679	4929	56800	64476	-250	-7676
Technicians And Associate Professionals	2010	1915	1760	25283	22872	155	2411
	2014	2802	2472	35547	32215	330	3332

Table 4.14: Continued

Gender Wage Gap							
Science And Engineering Associate Professionals	2010	1974	1812	26076	23200	162	2876
	2014	3108	2282	39131	28723	826	10408
Health Associate Professionals	2010	1526	1619	18952	19971	-93	-1019
	2014	2137	2137	26021	28123	0	-2102
Business And Administration Associate Professionals	2010	1792	1767	24157	23366	25	791
	2014	2498	2678	32041	34890	-180	-2849
Legal, Social, Cultural And Related Associate Professionals	2010	2108	1870	25336	22917	238	2419
	2014	3149	2832	39159	37074	317	2085
Information And Communications Technicians	2010	2355	1785	31922	23313	570	8609
	2014	2935	2982	39143	40201	-47	-1058
Clerical Support Workers	2010	1645	1531	22066	20700	114	1366
	2014	2111	1979	26700	25178	132	1522
General And Keyboard Clerks	2010	1436	1154	19110	14734	282	4376
	2014	2007	1619	25328	20237	388	5091
Customer Services Clerks	2010	2041	1944	29948	28341	97	1607
	2014	2604	2396	35196	31870	208	3326
Numerical And Material Recording Clerks	2010	1496	1407	19031	17715	89	1316
	2014	1986	1879	24517	23158	107	1359
Other Clerical Support Workers	2010	1638	1449	20848	18634	189	2214
	2014	2221	2275	27883	28759	-54	-876
Service And Sales Workers	2010	1122	1030	14076	12919	92	1157
	2014	1557	1432	19601	18152	125	1449
Personal Service Workers	2010	1066	940	13184	11884	126	1300
	2014	1548	1361	18801	16391	187	2410
Sales Workers	2010	1068	1059	13425	13332	9	93
	2014	1561	1454	19922	18699	107	1223
Personal Care Workers	2010	1124	1035	13647	12367	89	1280
	2014	1722	1440	21413	17691	282	3722

(*Continued*)

Table 4.14: Continued

Gender Wage Gap							
Protective Services Workers	2010	1310	1209	16680	14576	101	2104
	2014	1542	1465	19835	20944	77	-1109
Skilled Agricultural, Forestry And Fishery Workers	2010	-	-	-	-	-	-
	2014	1558	1216	17297	14151	342	3146
Market-Oriented Skilled Agricultural Workers	2010	-	-	-	-	-	-
	2014	1558	1216	20271	15412	342	4859
Craft And Related Trades Workers	2010	1320	1085	17297	14151	235	3146
	2014	1778	1413	21484	17274	365	4210
Building And Related Trades Workers, Excluding Electricians	2010	1026	984	13048	12825	42	223
	2014	1598	2361	19327	25639	-763	-6312
Metal, Machinery And Related Trades Workers	2010	1502	1697	19967	23280	-195	-3313
	2014	1992	1634	24244	20936	358	3308
Handicraft And Printing Workers	2010	1369	910	18701	11404	459	7297
	2014	1537	1433	18656	17405	104	1251
Electrical And Electronic Trades Workers	2010	1635	1404	20880	17359	231	3521
	2014	2106	1822	25365	22440	284	2925
Food Processing, Wood Working, Garment And Other Craft And Related Trades	2010	1095	1011	14067	13150	84	917
	2014	1552	1367	18572	16741	185	1831
Plant And Machine Operators, And Assemblers	2010	1159	875	15144	11266	284	3878
	2014	1717	1309	21056	16205	408	4851
Stationary Plant And Machine Operators	2010	1181	864	15751	11169	317	4582
	2014	1685	1277	20590	15585	408	5005
Assemblers	2010	1217	988	15183	12189	229	2994
	2014	2158	1525	25938	20271	633	5667
Drivers And Mobile Plant Operators	2010	-	-	-	-	-	-
	2014	1651	1657	20474	23128	-6	-2654
Elementary Occupations	2010	1048	892	13513	11276	156	2237
	2014	1428	1287	17515	15721	141	1794

Table 4.14: Continued

Gender Wage Gap							
Cleaners And Helpers	2010	979	876	12324	10810	103	1514
	2014	1397	1264	16841	15327	133	1514
Agricultural, Forestry And Fishery Labourers	2010	-	-	-	-	-	-
	2014	1528	1566	19132	19050	-38	82
Labourers In Mining, Construction, Manufacturing And Transport	2010	1066	901	13853	11706	165	2147
	2014	1432	1304	17633	16210	128	1423
Food Preparation Assistants	2010	1116	881	14417	11131	235	3286
	2014	1446	1317	17724	15853	129	1871
Street And Related Sales And Service Workers	2010	-	-	-	-	-	-
	2014	1403	1205	17997	14592	198	3405
Refuse Workers And Other Elementary Workers	2010	1018	1182	12982	14956	-164	-1974
	2014	1459	1362	18062	16750	97	1312

sectors and higher-paying titles the gap is at the vastest levels. Opposingly, in some professions which are conventionally thought of as feminine, men might receive less salary. However, the difference of pay gaps toward men and women is unmatched, since the discrepancy is a cliff. It is visible that the wage gap towards men has been reversed in three positions in 2014. Moreover, even they lead to a wage gap towards women. However, many institutions claim the contrary, that the issue is rising from other reasons.

Equal pay for equal work has been a human right since 1951 in ILO. Regardless of laws against pay difference, problems begin with transparency and implementation. Often the labor pays are not evaluated by the regulatory authorities. Henceforth, without regulations and accountability, it is just an encouragement for organizations to pay less. Disclosure of pay and combatting the secrecy over pay is necessary to observe the bias and prevent it. Thus, pay transparency, regulations and their implementation are the only essential tools to battle it.

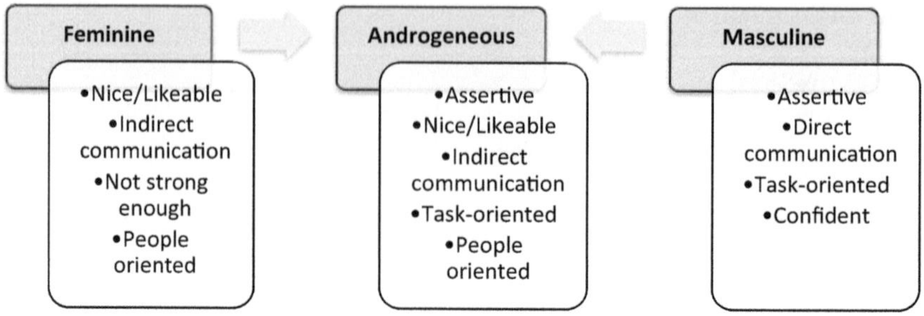

Figure 4.2: Gender in the leadership (Billing, 2011)

Cliff and the Maternalistic Leadership

Female managers are assumed to be motherly, forgiving, comfortable and good at team building. However, there is no evidence presenting behavioral differences among genders in a managerial position.

Gender is not explicit in-office communications. It is apparent as an invisible/glass culture. Therefore, most concepts on the topic start with glass because they can't be physically seen but felt. In which women are instantly affiliated with the supporting roles. Consequently, the capabilities of women managers are constantly in question (Wharton, 2012). Therefore, women find the solution in creating a more masculine work gender to gain access to the corporate ladder. By adding their gender to the required traits, they create a more androgynous and hybrid leadership style (Billing, 2011).

Another reason for this is, assertive behavior is not viewed as favorable and is often met with resistance due to this coding. Contrariwise, carrying feminine traits can be considered as "not tough enough" and as a weakness (Eagly & Carli, 2007, p. 123). This dilemma is called the "double-blind" (Billing, 2011).

Hence, androgynous leadership styles are not mutually exclusively identified as feminine or masculine. They mix "*assertive competence with supportive friendliness*" and alter it depending on the sector (Eagly & Carli, 2007, p. 123). Assertiveness is combined with indirect communication because disagreeing or deterrence can prevent raises and promotions for women. As a result, senior female managers spend most of their time communicating their agenda without backlashes from their counterparts and subordinates (Eagly & Carli, 2007).

Current trends in leadership are in favor of the teacherly method, which resonates more with femininity over command and control-based styles (Eagly & Carli, 2007). Maternal leadership is called in times of crisis. It has become a theme in recent years, instead of paternalistic. In New Zealand and Australia, women authorities received positive results compared to paternalistic countries in combatting Covid-19.

Harmoniously, prime ministers and other political animals are being replaced by women. Regularly, it would be considered as a positive development for political participation and leadership. However, the issue is the glass cliff, which emerges in times of crisis, putting womens' careers at risk. Overt examples of this are Margaret Thatcher and Theresa May. However, this trend ends right after the pandemic. This jeopardizing position for women, therefore, is considered as a cliff.

In 2021 number of women CEOs in the Fortune 500 companies has reached 41 (8 %). It was 33 and 24 in 2019 and 2018. Though there is an increase, 8 % is still dreadfully low for 2021. Newcomb mentions the preference towards female management during the crisis and the cliff making circumstances underneath it (Newcomb, 2020).

Conclusion

Working from home (WFH) might become permanent in some sectors, though it already existed in the IT sector. However, it is still early to make estimations for the future since organizations are trying to find their solutions, with the vaccinated employees, productivity, quarterly earnings and new variants and waves on whether to call the employees back.

Most organizations are changing their status, like Google and Morgan Stanley have. It looks like that a hybrid style of work might prevail in more flexible organizations and sectors. However, the disruption forces the work-life, the household division of labor and the power balance between the spouses (Hochschild & Machung, 2003).

Prevention of bias towards woman employees seems that ought to be the primary concern of organizations. For child-care, the PwC report illustrates the increasing burden from 6 hours to 7.7 hours per day makes it almost a full-time unpaid job.

Alternatively, men habitually are not considered as a gender. However, like in any stereotype, it hurts many who does not fit the frames written centuries ago. No person is born to be better at doing something than the other. Only the skills and experience make sure of that. Henceforward, equal pay focused incentives and enforcement policies ought to be targeted by politicians to involve the entire labor force. Diversity creates more harmony than coerced coherence, which eliminates challenges and evolution.

Although many organizations urged and preached for policies, interventions, and actions to prevent the increasing inequality between genders against the effects of Covid-19, there has been no evidence on actions taken. The pandemic will end, the inequality level will eventually and gradually return to its pre-pandemic levels. School drop-out rates were one of the primary issues in this period. It means that one generation of children and girls are harmed, which can't be reversed. UNCTAD states that with the pandemic, women's' rights lost 40 years of progression, the inequality gap has reached a new peak, 136 years (UNCTAD, 2021). In 2020, I witnessed such an instance. A girl was trying to convince her parents for a university education in tears. Education saves lives, factually and metaphorically. It affects the individual economically, socially, politically, and psychologically. Moreover, it helps in combatting certain aspects of the shadow pandemic. Therefore, a lot more needs to be done policy-wise to return to the pre-pandemic levels before it is too late.

Zülfiye Gül Ercan and Feyza Nazan Gündüz

Chapter 5 Pandemic and Early Childhood Education

Introduction

Twentieth century passed as a century that left profound effects on history in which two great world wars and economic crises took place, climate changes have started, because of the wars, some states were destroyed, and new states were established in their place, human beings experienced changes in sociological, psychological, political, economic, technological fields. Twenty-first century, on the other hand, differs from previous centuries in that the world has been experiencing unpredictably large and rapid changes. Changes that occurred slowly, cumulatively, and gradually in previous periods, took place in the first 20 years of the 21st century in the form of rapid and sharp breaks, and it is still happening. Especially the changes and advances taking place in technology are happening at a dizzying pace and are creating great changes in the life of mankind. For example, technology has increased transportation opportunities throughout the world and has made the world a global village that is easily accessible everywhere (Buluk & Eşitti, 2020). It has diversified and facilitated access to information, made possible things that seem impossible in areas such as health, engineering, and allows people to live more comfortable and faster lives. Enabling technology to open and accelerate new channels of access to information, has led the 21st century to be called the "information age" (İnci & Kandır, 2017). The rapid spread of knowledge and its reach to a wide audience constitute the necessity for different cultures to live together and adapt to each other. At the same time, while the information age provides humanity with new opportunities and conveniences, it also causes the rapid depletion of resources existing in many areas and the emergence of more resource needs. Climate change, ecological degradation, environmental pollution, the reduction in water and food resources has begun to change the structure of society, it has revealed the need to reshape societies by leading to migration, urbanization, income, social injustice, conflict, and instability, economic crises, populist policies.

For societies to be reformed, it is also necessary to develop the qualities of their members that they have. The 21st century reveals the fact that "man is at the center of progress and change, that investment must be made in man, and that what is important is how to process and use information rather than access it". Therefore, all societies/countries need individuals who can adapt to changes in a rapidly changing world, capture technology, select, analyze and evaluate information from among the information piles produced, and use this information in their daily lives, turn information into a product. And this can be achieved through education. Therefore, education is responsible for raising individuals who can cope with the problems posed by the new age and adapt to it in order to meet the demands of this century (Aygün, Atalay, Kılıç & Yaşar, 2016; Tuğluk & Özkan, 2019).

Being able to become an information society in the information age in which we live has become one of the main goals of all countries, and countries have begun to prioritize educating their citizens. Because staying out of the developments in information and information technologies makes it impossible to exist and maintain it in the international arena, to compete, and also makes societies and countries dependent on others. Twenty-first century has brought about the need to produce and benefit from science more than ever before. Therefore, it has become necessary for several changes in educational systems and institutions in order to educate qualified individuals who are required by the new age. For example, changes include strengthening the technological infrastructure in education, establishing new schools, increasing the number of classrooms, updating educational programs, moving learning spaces not only to school buildings, but also outside the school to different places (forest schools, outdoor learning areas, home education, etc.), making distance education (e-learning) systems effective and widespread, making changes in learning times, etc. (Tuğluk & Özkan, 2019; Tutkun & Aksoyalp, 2010; Yalçın, Simsar & Dinler, 2020).

Pandemic and Education

On March 11, 2020, a pandemic was declared by the World Health Organization, also called a global epidemic worldwide (WHO, 2020). During the pandemic process that occurred, countries asked their citizens to "Stay at Home!". To reduce the spread of the virus and prevent the collapse of the health system, restrictions and quarantine practices have been implemented in various areas internationally and nationally around the world. Except for the institutions that serve to meet basic needs such as cleaning, health, nutrition, almost all public and private institutions were closed to prevent the spread of the virus, curfews were put, social activities were stopped, schools were closed and education was implemented through distance learning, working from home system to avoid contact with each other was launched. This unexpected and rapid change has negatively affected people's lives (Giannini & Lewis, 2020; Kurt Demirtaş & Sevgili Koçak, 2020).

The COVID-19 pandemic first emerged in Turkey on March 11, 2020, and the first death due to the epidemic occurred on March 18, 2020. After this date, various restrictions were taken to reduce the rate of spread of the disease throughout the country and eliminate the epidemic. A total curfew has been imposed for individuals aged 65 and over who are considered a risk group, and for individuals aged 20 and under. Individuals who are outside these ages are also prohibited from going outside except in cases that require necessity. On May 4, 2020, the gradual normalization calendar was announced and started to be implemented throughout the country. According to the Covid 19 case numbers, death, transmission and vaccination rates, the course of closure and mandatory quarantine practices has been shaped throughout the country or at the local level (Aykar & Yurdakal, 2021; Toran, 2021).

In this process, it has become mandatory to switch to distance education in order to be able to continue educational activities without interruption and to prevent children from falling behind in education. In the process of this unusual pandemic all over the world, it is aimed to achieve educational activities quickly and reliably (Hodges, Moore, Lockee, Trust & Bond, 2020). Various countries have provided distance education services to teachers and students through television and the Internet using information communication technologies. For example, the People's Republic of China, has started the process of distance education with online platform options under the coordination of the Ministry of Education and the Ministry of Information Technology (Xie & Yang, 2020), Czechia, on the other hand, via television and the Internet (Brom, Lukavský, Greger, Hannemann, Straková, & Švarícek, 2020).

On March 12, 2020, all social events in schools were canceled in our country, and schools were on vacation from March 16, 2020 to March 30, 2020. During this holiday period, online professional work has been organised for school administrators and teachers. As the epidemic began to spread throughout the country, the Ministry of National Education (MEB) the Higher Education Institution (YÖK) decided that schools would not be opened in the spring semester (MEB, 2020a; YÖK, 2020). After the decision, distance education was quickly started at the primary, middle and high school levels, except for the pre-school level. Distance education has started via TRT EBA TV and EBA infra-structure. Students were able to follow their courses asynchronously via EBA. For students who do not have access to the EBA and do not have computer and/or internet access at home, the same courses were broadcast at certain times of the day on TRT channels. Thanks to this, students who do not have internet and computer access, but have a television at home, have also been able to follow their classes. Universities, on the other hand, have quickly become involved in the process with web televisions and various internet applications over the web. Since then, about 25 million students and more than one and a half billion students worldwide have switched from formal education to distance education (Konca & Cakır, 2021; Sak, Sahin Sak & Nas, 2020, pp. 161–189; Sirer, 2020; UNESCO, 2021).

Distance education, which dates to the 19th century, is defined as the continuation of education that cannot be carried out face to face for various reasons, by means of media communication tools without any interruption. Previously, it was carried out by transmitting printed educational materials to students, while it has been carried out by presenting educational content through television and computer with the participation of visual media tools in daily life in the 21st century (Kiryakova, 2009; Akkas Baysal, Ocak & Ocak, 2020). With the development of technology, distance education has started to provide its users learning activities through digital education platforms in electronic environment with their fast and rich contents (Altıparmak, 2011, pp. 319–327). Although the distance education model was previously used in higher education, in programs aimed at personal development and career development, by 21st century, it has been used at the primary and secondary levels of education (İnan-Kaya, 2021), and with the Covid-19 pandemic, it has started to be used compulsorily in all educational institutions from preschool to higher education (Akkaş Baysal et al., 2020).

The Covid-19 pandemic has deeply shaken the systems that countries have established with long-term cumulative knowledge and experience. Many economic, political, social, and other systems, especially health and education, have reached the point of collapse or have undergone a major transformation. Even in the recent past, many applications and experiences that can be considered utopian have started to emerge (Bozkurt, 2020; Sangster, Stoner, & Flood, 2020). Countries that are more economically powerful and can create the necessary infrastructure to bring technology to education have adapted easily to the distance education process with the closure of schools. Countries that cannot make this investment, on the other hand, have not been able to adapt or have struggled. Although it provides great opportunities for educators and students, distance education has prerequisites. For example, access to distance education requires infrastructure and technological devices for users. To be used throughout the society, the infrastructure and equipment must be widespread and easily accessible. Otherwise, it can only be used by a certain segment of society. A thorough planning and preparation is required. Because it has many different components, it is a multidisciplinary education. Distance education should be user-friendly, be able to offer alternatives rich in content and materials, be suitable for reorganization. Distance education aims to create a long-term sustainable learning ecosystem and is constantly updated with feedback from users about the process, content and applications. Another issue is how users will prepare for this process. For example, the competencies of educators and students related to the use of technological devices, the ability to learn-use digital educational platforms, interactive processing of education in virtual classrooms, providing educators with skills related to virtual classroom management are of the important issues (Bozkurt et al., 2020; Can, 2020; Iwai, 2020; Muhdi, & Yuliejantiningsih, 2020; Sezgin, 2021).

To reduce the spread and deadly effects of the Covid-19 pandemic, rapidly closing countries have rapidly switched to distance education to prevent individuals from getting the right to education and minimize the inequality of opportunity in education. Face-to-face education in normal conditions has temporarily led to alternative options due to a crisis such as a pandemic. This educational response, called emergency distance education, has quickly responded to the educational negativity brought about by the pandemic process (Ak, Gökdaş, Öksüz, & Torun, 2021; Bozkurt et al., 2020; Ferri, Grifoni & Guzzo, 2020; Hodge, Moore, Lockee, Trust & Bond, 2020). In a very short period, educators and students came together with the help of various online technologies. In this process, urgent distance education has tried to compensate for the gaps and losses that may occur and occur in education, rather than offering distance education, which is ideal. He offered a temporary educational support to educators and students (Hodges et al., 2020; Sezgin, 2021).

The urgent process of distance education has caused educators to experience problems and concerns such as developing content, finding the right technologies, learning, and using them. On the other hand, access to digital platforms that have started to be used in this process, the capacity of the platforms, concerns about the protection and use of personal data during use have also created resistance and reluctance to distance education. In this process, adapting to this new system in almost all segments of society has led to the fact that the screen has been extended, because of which the daily life routines have changed, and even preparing for the lesson for educators, being able to explain the lesson has become a primary priority. Although online trainings are offered to school administrators and educators urgently at the beginning of the process, these trainings are mostly about introducing digital platforms, how to implement distance education, how to make student evaluations, etc. Educators have not received adequate training on how technology can be adapted to pedagogical content, how they can practice with students in a classroom setting. This, in turn, influenced the readiness of educators and students, their attitude to distance education, the effectiveness and efficiency of distance education. For example, the self-efficacy of educators in teaching on digital platforms, their motivation, have affected the ability to manage their virtual classrooms, the participation of students in the lesson, and their willingness to perform lesson-related tasks. The ability of students to use technological devices, the ability to choose and manage their own learning processes and educational materials also influenced the attitude and behavior of educators to the process of thinking about it. From another point of view, it seems that the new educational habits, experiences, and lifestyle brought about by the urgent distance education process have had and will have an impact on distance or face-to-face education activities in the new normalization process (Bozkurt et al., 2020; Sarıtaş & Barutçu, 2020; Sezgin, 2021).

Early Childhood Education in the Pandemic Process

Starting from June 1, 2020, the gradual normalization process has been started, and state and public institutions have switched to normal working patterns. With the end of the homework system, parents have started to search for both the care and education of their children. First of all, it was decided to open private Kindergartens and Day Care Centers affiliated to the Ministry of Family, Labor and Social Services (AÇSHB), then only private kindergartens and kindergartens affiliated to the Ministry of Education and Training, provided that parents with children first comply with the protocols against the epidemic in accordance with the requests and requests of institutions that will provide care for their children, and a few weeks later, the schools went on summer vacation. After the summer break, face-to-face training was started in all public and private institutions, On September 21st, preschool and primary school levels started their education for one day and from September 28th for two days, the number of students in the classes was halved and as of October 12, 2020, five days of training were started on weekdays. distance learning was started again from November 20, 2020, to January 4, 2021, with the increase in cases. In this process, distance education was carried out before the school through various sharing sites with the individual efforts of its teachers, and then TRT EBA TV, EBA portal and other reliable open-source platforms. MEB has also offered a psychosocial support package through EBA to reduce the traumatic effects of COVID-19 on preschool and elementary school students. As of January 4, 2021, the schools were opened face to face again and educational services were carried out face to face five days a week, especially at the levels of early childhood education and care (Akkaş Baysal et al., 2020; Sak et al., 2020).

Distance education for preschool education is a new situation. In most of the available information about preschool education, it is recommended that education in this period be offered face-to-face, in educational institutions and educational settings organized for children, based on the most ideal applications of existing educational approaches for the child. The child's creative and critical thinking skills by trying to give the child a chance to learn, to gain different experiences to enable children to ensure the active participation of the family and individual differences and requirements are being focused on. In the education provided to the child, activities are presented in a planned and systematic way, the educational environment is designed according to the interests and needs of developmental characteristics, all developmental areas of the child are supported by providing rich stimuli, and equal opportunities are aimed at children from disadvantaged environments (Ministry of National Education, 2013). As a matter of fact, the results obtained from various studies show that a qualified preschool education increases the social adaptation, cognitive, affective and psychomotor development of children in direct proportion to the education they receive (Erkan & Kırca, 2010; Metin & Aral, 2016), it turns out that it affects the personality structure, habits, values and beliefs, and even these effects last until the end of life (Currie & Almond, 2011; Heckman, Pinto & Savelyev, 2013). Skalicka, Belsky, Stenseng, and Wichstrøm (2015) have stated that children who are not close with pre-school teachers, and with social problems, have been experiencing more conflict with teachers in primary education, however, the problematic behaviors seen before school continue during the primary education period.

However, the Covid-19 pandemic has caught the education systems unprepared as well as the whole world. Pre-school education with technological infrastructure, digital content, and human resources (legislators, educators, administrators, parents) with was caught unprepared. The fact that many schools and preschool teachers do not have enough knowledge and experience in this regard has made the situation even more difficult. To prevent young students from being cut off from school and education during the pandemic process, and to allow them to pass this process more psychologically, urgent distance education has been started, which will be adapted to various face-to-face educational content and applications. However, before the pandemic, while the problems such as war, migration, etc. threaten the equality of opportunity in education, the transition to urgent distance education in the pandemic process has increased the inequality of opportunity in education, and the growth of economic problems has deepened the gap (Can, 2020; Muhdi & Yuliejantiningsih, 2020).

Teachers during Pandemic

Teachers are the main actors in the use of technological tools and materials in education. Teachers who have sufficient skills in using technology, who can make the right choice about software, who have the experience to prepare the technological materials they need, who can be aware that technology is a tool and not a goal in education and training, improve the quality of education. Because these teachers can use their excitement and desires in an educational way by directing children's interest in technological tools to education (Cabı, 2018; Kol, 2012; Yılmazsoy, Özdinç & Kahraman, 2018). With the turn of the 21st century, the digitalization movement in education has begun, and this change and transformation has been implemented by all stakeholders at almost every level of education. Early childhood education institutions have also tried to keep up with technological adaptation. Preschool teachers have started to use technological adaptation for integrative purposes in face-to-face education. Technological adaptation at the preschool age began with educational films, videos, and recently games that develop intelligence have been used in various activities such as group games played by multiple users, digital storytelling, and so on. Many studies also emphasize that this technological adaptation in preschool age contributes to the development of skills such as visual literacy, helpfulness, technological competence, creativity, and problem solving (Heo, 2009; Robin, 2008).

However, the education carried out face to face with the Covid 19 pandemic had to turn into an emergency distance education model at once. Teachers who conduct training with their students in their classrooms have quickly moved to virtual classrooms, have evolved into teachers who can share screens, work on a common screen. As a result of this evolution, teachers have taken on responsibilities such as preparing digital content, sharing digital content, using technological devices in student tracking and measurement evaluation systems. In addition, they had to perform tasks such as managing the virtual classroom in the educational process, reaching the student, adding them to the education, directing them to use an informed screen, communicating correctly through technology (Akkaş Baysal et al., 2020; Aykar & Yurdakal, 2021).

Most preschool teachers have emphasized that young children and pre-school education in some ways is not suitable for the practices of distance education, pre-school education in the use of technology should be used in a supportive and complementary manner. In particular, it has been stated that it should be noted that the developmental characteristics and needs of children (play, movement, social emotional development, interaction with peers, etc.) that cannot be fully covered by distance education, while some activities in educational applications (large group activities, game and movement activities, activities that support self-care skills, activities that support communication skills, etc.) will not be possible to transfer it to digital media.

It has been stated by teachers that they do not have enough knowledge and experience for a qualified distance education. Jonassen bases the failure of teachers to use technology on their inability to find time, not being well trained in how to use technology, lack of technical support, imposition of technology use on teachers (Orçan-Kaçan & Kimzan, 2017). However, Lavidas et al. (2021) stated that preschool teachers have a satisfactory self-efficacy for information communication technologies integration. Teachers note that they do not have an idea of how to prepare for distance education for families and children, as they have not been through any mediation process. Factors such as access to the Internet, access to and use of technological devices, decisiveness of appropriate digital platforms, digital educational resources, difficulties in adapting some educational materials to the distance learning process, individual differences between children, material deficiencies prevent the implementation of distance education. For example, the lack of devices that ensure the availability of the Internet, the frequent disconnection of the Internet, the inability to transfer educational content to a digital platform, the inability to properly use technological devices prevent the teacher from carrying out the planned training. It also causes inequality of opportunity in education (Aykar & Yurdakal, 2021; Iwai, 2020; Muhdi & Yuliejantiningsih, 2020; Yıldırım, 2021). A large part of the teachers also accept the fact that the pandemic is an exceptional situation and that a quick transition should be made to ensure that education is not disrupted (Muhdi & Yuliejantiningsih, 2020).

Teachers talk about the periods when families reflect their problems that have developed due to the pandemic on the educational process, their attitudes and behavior. They stated that this situation causes families to be disconnected from education by preventing them from participating in the educational process or by creating emotional pressure on the child. Teachers ensure that families provide support to the child and teacher when their child is involved in the educational process, while showing an indifferent attitude can lead to a decrease in the child's success. Parents have occasionally agreed to allow unlimited access to technological tools to control their child's behavior at home, which can cause problems in the development areas of children (Aral & Doğan- Keskin, 2018; Sapsağlam, 2018).

Social media platforms have become a place where both teachers and families can have a dialogue, share ideas and information about digital materials related to education, and use them to solve common problems. Thus, phones, tablets and computers have become tools that can produce solutions without wasting time (Aykar &Yurdakal, 2021).

Families during Pandemic

Mankind has experienced many disasters since his existence and has survived these disasters both physically and spiritually as a unity. Now, to get rid of the Covid-19 pandemic that threatens humanity, people are trying to isolate themselves from each other, act jointly against the disease, and adapt to new conditions. The main feature that also distinguishes the Covid-19 pandemic from other disasters is the decommissioning or minimization of contact between people. A worldwide quarantine has been declared to prevent the spread of the disease, eliminate its deadly effects, and protect against the disease. Quarantine practices have completely changed the life of mankind. At the first stage, workplaces were closed, social activities were banned, it was switched on flexible working order and emergency distance education (Karakaş, 2020; Tunç & Atıcı, 2020).

Losing someone from within the family or from the family circle due to an epidemic, fear of contracting an epidemic, effort to protect against the disease, uncertainty about the course of the epidemic, having to close home, changing daily routines, work and economic concerns have negatively affected the family life and structure have created both pressure and physical-spiritual burnout on the parents (Kurt Demirtaş & Sevgili Koçak, 2020). Parents who continue to work from home with a flexible working form have experienced several difficulties in protecting and maintaining a balance between work and family dynamics. The boundaries and balances between work and home life have completely changed. The inability of people who care for the child, other than the parents, to come home has increased the burden of the parents even more. With the transition to distance education, parents have taken on the role of teacher in addition to the role of home parenting for their children. Da Silva, Lordello, Schmidt, and Mietto de Melo (2020) have stated the biggest challenges their families have faced in the pandemic as to deal with more than one task at home, to show interest in children, create a routine, play with the kids on various topics that can convince kids to make comments, share tasks and assist with school activities (Da Silva et al., 2020). It was determined that families with young children preferred household routines where they take part with their children and mobile games / activities, table activities which they play together with their children. Parents do not have the energy for mobile games/activities because of working from home due to flexible working, the change of responsibilities at work and at home, financial worries, increased workloads. Studies have found that activities performed at home include playing brain teasers, reading stories before sleep, helping with household chores, and doing school homeworks (Kurt Demirtaş & Sevgili Koçak, 2020; Kundu & Bhowmik, 2020).

During the pandemic process, studies on distance education in Turkey started from April 1, 2020, at the first stage, distance education was started at primary, middle and high school levels, except for the preschool level. Activity resources, manuals have been prepared for schools, teachers, parents and children and are intended to be delivered to interested parties until the gradual normalization period is started as of June 1, 2020. With a Gradual return to normal on June 1, 2020, Private Nurseries and Day Care Centers affiliated to the Ministry of Family, Labor and Social Services were opened with the requirement to comply with the protocols against the epidemic, after that, private kindergartens and kindergartens affiliated to the Ministry of Education were opened (Sak et al., 2020, p. 161–189). However, the opening of schools has not been able to ensure that children in preschool age benefit from educational services. At that time, 1,340,507 children out of 1,629,720 children did not benefit from early childhood education and care services. After the summer holidays, the necessary measures were taken and on September 21, the preschool education and primary school levels were started to be trained one day a week, two days a week from September 28, and five days from October 12, 2020 (Sak et al., 2020, pp. 161–189). However, with the increase in cases, it was switched to distance learning again from November 20, 2020 to January 4, 2021, and education and training services were carried out on TRT EBA TV, EBA portal and other reliable open source platforms (MEB, 2020b).

With the transition to distance education, many problems have arisen for families. In the first stage, economic problems have taken a leading role in accessing distance education. The need for internet infrastructure, tablet, or computer or even television has arisen for participation in the courses. In families with more than one child attending school, the number of computers or tablets has become insufficient due to the fact that the children's class hours coincide, with the simultaneous access of many technological devices to the Internet, the speed of Internet access has decreased, in some places, access to the Internet was never provided and it was not possible for children to participate in distance education. All these factors have further deepened the inequality of opportunities in education (Toran, 2021). For children of preschool age, this situation becomes a little more difficult. Because children of this age group can attend classes with the help of an adult. For this, parents should be available and involve the child in the lesson. This situation poses a problem for working parents. The skills of older parents to use technological devices and the Internet enable or prevent the young child from participating in education. Because classes are conducted on the basis of activity in preschool education, it is necessary to prepare and follow the materials required for participation in the lesson by adults (Akkaş Baysal et al., 2020). The fact that children are young also makes it difficult for them to adapt to the lesson. Since they are easily distracted, guidance and intervention of adults are needed from time to time. In addition to their parenting roles, families also had to take on the role of assistant teachers during the pandemic process (Toran, Sak, Xu, & Şahin-Sak veYu, 2021).

Parents' educational levels and digital literacy may affect their beliefs and attitudes about distance education. Parents can shape children's skills in using technological devices. The fact is that parents will be able to benefit more from education and technology when their children can use digital tools and equipment appropriately. Children will be able to use technological devices, access and use appropriate contents. They will be able to be equipped against the dangers of the digital world. As parents' education levels increase, they can become more of a role model and offer guidance to their children. These parents accompany their children more often when using technological devices and use the guidance approach more when learning these technologies and evaluating the content. They can warn and protect their children against dangers and risks in the digital world. On the other hand, parents may be concerned about the risks of their children using the Internet, using technological tools, and accessing digital content. They limit their children from accessing the Internet and using technological devices, especially if they do not know enough about the risks, they are unable to guide their children in this regard. On the other hand, children of families with low socioeconomic status can access inappropriate digital content that they can use these tools more often without parental supervision and guidance (İnan-Kaya, 2021).

Children during the Pandemic

Today's children are opening their eyes to a world dominated by technology. Children in early childhood are curious and interested in their environment and technological products as of the period they are in. While many children can't even express themselves anymore, they encounter digital tools such as computers, smartphones, tablets in their daily lives, communication, games and learning activities (İnci & Kandır, 2017). According to statistics, it has been determined that 4 billion 540 million of the 7 billion 750 million people in the world use the Internet. Children and teenagers also make up a third of these users. Experts note that the use of the Internet will also gradually increase (Sirer,

2020; We Are Social Digital, 2020). In his study investigating the screen exposure times of children, Tuğrul (2019) found that children are on average at the screen for 2 hours and 18 minutes a day, 40 % of these children use only the television screen, 60 % are exposed to the screen using social media such as YouTube, 39 % Facebook, and 24 % WhatsApp. The researcher also noted that the time spent in front of the screen is quite a lot for the age and developmental level of children. The fact that technological devices provide content such as colorful visuals, moving pictures, animations, videos keep children's curiosity, creativity, independence, and enthusiasm to explore alive. With these features, digital devices such as smartphones and tablets become an integral part of the games, social lives, communication and learning of young children. It provides children with more fun and lasting learning, reinforcement opportunities and opportunities to correct incorrect learning (Uluser-İnan, 2003; Özyürek, 2018). Some researchers point out that technological tools and digital educational content contribute to young children's understanding and learning of abstract concepts-information, that it also supports the development of collaborative learning, problem solving and reasoning skills. Technological devices also give children the opportunity to choose their own way of learning. While children in preschool age learn both by visual and auditory means, at the primary or later stages of education, children can choose to learn by visual or auditory means according to their preferences. These devices also provide quiet, introverted, timid students who have difficulty expressing themselves in the classroom during face-to-face training with the opportunity to participate in distance education in their own comfortable spaces. Studies have shown that the use of technology positively supports children's learning and increases their motivation, learning with a screen leads to a 91 % increase in student satisfaction and an 82 % increase in children's achievements (Akkaş Baysal et al., 2020; Çakıroğlu & Taşkın, 2016; Dong, Cao & li, 2020; Huffstetter, King, Onwuegbuzie, Schneider, & Powell-Smith, 2010; İnci & Kandır, 2017; Jones, 2020; Kocaman-Karoğlu, 2016; Sirer, 2020; Şahin, 2006; Wolgemuth et al., 2011).

Preschool children who were included in distance education during the pandemic need to join groups of friends, adapt to school and class, develop social skills due to their developmental characteristics. However, children who were forced to stay at home during the Covid-19 pandemic remained away from school life and other social interactions that they maintained with their peers. It has been suggested that this isolation poses a direct risk to the physical, social, and psychological well-being of children, and even that the cognitive and emotional development of children is negatively affected due to the stress associated with the epidemic (Di Giorgio, Di Riso, Mioni & Cellini, 2020; Döğer & Kılınç, 2021).

To reduce the traumatic effects of COVID-19 on preschool and primary school students, the Ministry of National Education in Turkey has made various publications aimed at providing psychosocial support through the EBA. In addition, to ensure that children in the preschool period do not break away from education and training, physical, psychological and social emotional well-being, it has been switched to distance education. However, at the beginning of this transition, distance education applications for young children were provided by the personal means and efforts of preschool teachers, after that, activities suitable for the development of children for teachers and families were created and presented through TRT EBA Kindergarten (Toran, 2021).

One of the important reasons why distance education cannot be transferred to preschool education at the same time as other levels of education is that development is fast and multifaceted, and it is believed that these distance education contents in preschool period cannot be as effective and efficient as face-to-face education. It is important for children in this age group to learn using all their senses, gain experience by doing and living, gain social skills by role-modeling adults, older children, and peers through planned activities in organized educational environments suitable for their development. In addition, the pandemic has limited children's opportunities to play and discouraged them. However, children try to find opportunities to play anytime, anywhere and use any instrument as a toy. Playing is an important tool for understanding new concepts, making new discoveries about themselves and their environment, solving problems they face, using their imagination and creativity. In addition, motor skills, concentration, coordination and communication skills are being developed through the game (Solekhah, 2020). Some game events can be played alone. In some games, friends or peers are required. Such games serve more for the social emotional development of children. Like, belonging to a group, following the rules of the group and the game, knowing how to win and lose, learning how to compete, taking responsibility, taking initiative, etc. Although children have various opportunities to play games in the home environment, these facilities do not always meet the needs of the child.

Classroom environments controlled by teachers allow children to correct mistakes they have made in the learning process more easily. In addition, it is an environment where the skills that should have been acquired for social life are practiced. The child tries to behave as he should in real life with his experiences here. Considering all these factors, it is considered that distance education for preschool children may be limited and insufficient. Social interactions are recognized as the main components of early childhood experience. For meaningful learning to take place, the necessity of children's interaction with each other, children's communication with the teacher and children's communication with the content is clearly seen. In some studies, it is emphasized that effective results can be achieved by ensuring quality educational communication, correctly configuring educational technology and training, such as in face-to-face training (Akbaş & Dursun, 2020; Bozkurt, 2020). In this study, which was mentioned in the pandemic period, by contrast, needs more socialization of children, the movement needs are not being met, distance education courses that are offered by have difficulty in sitting in front of the screen, exhibit attention problems, emotionally negatively affected. It has been determined that the inability to attend school, the exclusion from social life increases the duration of internet and social media use, participation in online games, and leads to the conduct of course and extracurricular activities from the digital world (King et al., 2020; Wang et al., 2020; Witt et al., 2020; Yıldırım, 2021).

Döğer and Kılınç (2021) determined that although online education is thought to increase children's tablet, phone, and television usage, children use these devices most to watch cartoons, watch videos, and play games. The researcher noted that the fact that parents receive help from these devices in the distraction of their children in the process of home life also leads to this result. Çaykuş and Çaykuş (2020) attribute this to the fact that children have to participate in distance education activities without going through a specific orientation process and adapt to the process without receiving support.

Another factor is that families at home are turning more to screens for information about their work, life and the course of the epidemic. In the early days of the pandemic, Covid-19 transmission, those who died due to the disease, the state of hospitals, news about how to protect themselves from the disease, discussion programs, etc. it attracts the attention of children and leads to an increase in their anxiety and fear of the epidemic. This situation leads to the fact that children whose reasoning skills are not yet fully developed believe in all kinds of news. In the name of "learning", children's screen time increases, young children learn to passively accept the content offered to them, and some content that is considered educational does not give children something, it also negatively affects their psychological state (Sirer, 2020; Toran, 2021).

Conclusion and Recommendations

After the announcement of the Covid-19 pandemic, all countries of the world quickly closed to reduce the spread and deadly effects of the virus. In order not to impede the right of individuals to receive education and to minimize the inequality of opportunities in education, countries have switched to distance education to the extent possible. Face-to-face training in normal conditions has temporarily turned to alternative options due to a crisis such as a pandemic. This educational response, called urgent distance education, has quickly responded to the educational negativity brought about by the pandemic process. In a very short period, educators, students and even families have come together with the help of various online technologies. In countries that can invest in distance education, this transition has been easier and more acceptable. The studies conducted have revealed that during the transition to distance education, there are problems in education policies in existing education systems and in the dimension of teachers, families, and children, which are the most important elements of education.

In this section, which discusses the impact of the pandemic on preschool age, studies on preschool education, preschool teachers, young children, and their families have been examined and an attempt has been made to present a perspective on this issue. By legislators, educators, educators, academics and many field experts, early childhood is recognized as a critical period for the support and development of all areas of development of children. For this reason, it is necessary to focus on the importance of preschool education, to plan it meticulously for young children according to their age, interest in their development and needs, and to provide children with experiences that they can gain by living by doing.

The Covid-19 pandemic, which has led to the transformation of existing systems in the world, has also led to a transformation in early childhood education and has started to be offered to children through a distance education model. This transformation has attracted attention to issues such as technological infrastructure issues at all levels of education including pre-school education, including the way teachers, students, and families to compile the digital educational content of the preparation, the way to adapt existing training materials, the management of virtual classrooms, the student's participation, monitoring, evaluation in the lesson. Studies have shown that educators believe that the use of technology before school has a supportive and integrative nature of education, facilitates and accelerates it by embodying abstract content.

Both educators and families have experienced problems in realizing the prerequisites for distance education and have stated that if the necessary interventions are not made, it will lead to an inequality of opportunities in education. They also stated that some activities that can take place in face-to-face education cannot be carried out in distance education, and that they should be carried out face-to-face due to the developmental characteristics, needs and interests of the child.

Due to the continued uncertainty about the pandemic process and the determination of isolation conditions according to the course and severity of the pandemic, face-to-face training should be organized and structured in as much detail as distance education. It should be embraced that face-to-face, distance and hybrid education models can be used at all levels of education. The following suggestions can be presented in the light of the findings obtained from the literature review.

- It may be recommended that infrastructure arrangements be made during the distance education process and that solutions to problems that may arise in the process be completed before the process begins.
- Distance education is an educational model that has many components. In addition to the infrastructure regulations, it can be recommended that both its planning and implementation and its legislation be prepared well.
- Including not only educators, but also managers, families, and children in distance education orientation activities will increase the quality of distance education. Families should be provided with trainings on how they can guide their children through the distance education process. Trainings should contain examples of adaptation and application rather than the introduction of distance education and should be aimed at gaining experience.
- Distance education can create educational opportunities for groups that cannot benefit from face-to-face training. In other words, it serves to access people's right to education. Ensuring its accessibility will serve to access the right to education for many people.
- To create an alternative in education, in order not to be caught unprepared for possible disasters in the future, such as the Covid 19 pandemic, it is necessary to expand distance education, strengthen it and ensure that it is accessible to everyone.
- Distance education can be the model that can best support face-to-face education for preschool education. Priority should be given to the acceleration and dissemination of work on hybrid education in preschool education.
- The reasons for the reflection of the problems arising in the process of distance education on education should be determined and measures should be taken to address this situation.

Özlem Dağ

Chapter 6 Digital Transformation in Education After Covid-19

Introduction

The advances in science and technology have changed the world in the last 50 years. The COVID-19 epidemic turned this process to much more radical and faster. This pandemic is much more than a health crisis. It has changed every country, causing social, economic, and political crises that will leave devastating and deep scars. The rules of the game will change in the near and far future. New professions, new ways of production, new economic and political-social relations will have great effects. Society must change and transform. This is a new world.

Schools of the Future

The COVID-19 pandemic has led to a very rapid and unprecedented shift towards online education and digital technologies. Not in the future, but today, it is not a choice for schools to change their paradigm and integrate with technology to provide qualified education to provide the knowledge and skills needed by the new world order.

Education's Answer to the Covid-19 Crisis

"Digital Education Action Plan" was studied by the European Commission. (European Union, 2021), More than 2,700 participants from 60 countries were involved in discussions. About 60 % of the respondents stated that they did not use distance and online learning before the pandemic. Sixty-two percentage of those surveyed stated that they improved their Digital skills during the crisis. More than 50 % of respondents plan to act to further develop their Digital skills. Ninety-five percentage of respondents think the coronavirus crisis is a turning point in how digital technology is used in education and training.

World Scale Access to Distance Education

Around 1.2 billion children were affected by school closures as part of national and local quarantine measures. "Distance Education Accessibility Report" by UNICEF (UNICEF, 2020), emphasizes the restrictions brought by and major inequalities encountered in accessing distance education were discussed. The report includes the results of a research conducted around the world on the access of preschool, primary, secondary, and high school children to the in-home technological opportunities and tools they need to continue their distance education. The research, which has worldwide validity, was carried out by collecting data from 100 countries. Within the scope of the research, data were collected on television, radio, and internet access, and whether the curriculum was presented through these platforms during the closure of schools.

Seventy-two percentage of school-age children from the poorest households worldwide cannot access live distance education. In upper and middle-income countries, the proportion of school-aged children from the poorest households who cannot access distance education can reach up to 86 %. Three-quarters of school-age children living in rural areas around the world do not have access to live distance education opportunities.

Digital Transformation

Transition to distance education in Turkey started as of March 23, 2020. Distance digital education has been rapidly transitioned at all levels from kindergarten to graduate education. The volume of students according to the data announced by the Ministry of National Education (Selçuk, Z., 2020), a total of 18 million 108 thousand 860 students at pre-school, primary and secondary education levels, 8 million 240 thousand 997 students according to the statistics of the Higher Education Council (Higher Education Information Management System., 2020) been having in school classes in Turkey. All instruments of educational system were challenged by such strong questions:

- How to transform human resources to lead the digital education strategies?
- Direction of the transformation of educational philosophy?
- How to develop educational technologies?

Human Resources – Leading Digital Transformation

The Digital Teacher is the one who use digital tools and resources to accelerate and track their own professional development: reflect on their teaching, discover online conferences and sources of information, and share knowledge and best practice through a network of peers. The one who provide both opportunities and challenges for learning: evaluate, choose, and integrate digital tools and resources to support course aims and learning objectives, plan logical sequences of work for lessons and courses, and create attractive and useful interactive resources which maximize learning potential.

Transformation of Educational Philosophy

Digital transformation in education is not only the development of educational technologies. We are talking about a holistic change in the philosophy of education. For this reason, every teacher, especially education administrators, should play an encouraging role as a digital education leader.

Digital Education Philosophy

Philosophy is one of the ancient Greek society's three pillars, having emerged after the institutionalization of pedagogy and politics, which meant education for citizenship in the polis. Philosophy, politics, and pedagogy, particularly in relation to the demos and democratic values. Particularly crucial digital-age issues like communal intelligence, collaborative action, co-construction, and co-design of democratic commodities. Philosophy as pedagogy indicates that philosophy is dependent on the dialogue's educational forms. It is crucial for education because education is not only a discipline often conceived as the study of education with an emphasis on improvement, but also a massive enterprise, growing in importance in the knowledge economy, where such improvements are now driven by both economic theories about the importance of technology and technological innovations touted to transform its development. (Peters M.A.; Jandric P., 2015).

Digitalization is bringing becoming cyber civils. Learning to engage compassionately with others using stories is a great pedagogical practice that can occur at home or in the classroom.

Digital Pedagogy

During current pandemic, responsive and resilient pedagogy became a vivid need. The concept of digital pedagogy enters our lives at this point. Digital Pedagogy is more than just using digital technologies for teaching and learning; it is also about approaching digital tools from a critical pedagogical standpoint. As a result, it is as much about using digital tools thoughtfully as it is about deciding when not to use digital tools and paying attention to the impact of digital tools on learning.

Covid-19 Outbreak and Digital Transformation Opportunities in Education

The Covid-19 pandemic has created a range of education challenges, not just to public health, but to many other areas of activity including education. The need to contain the spread of the pandemic led many governments to put in place measures limiting physical proximity. In many cases this constrained the ability of students and teachers to meet in schools, as they normally would. Sustaining education continuity amidst this pandemic has been challenging around the world. To assist education leaders in those efforts the OECD (OECD, 2020) and the Global Education Innovation Initiative at Harvard University have collaborated to obtain and analyze information on the education conditions faced in countries, and on the approaches adopted to sustain educational opportunity. Respected scholars Andreas Schleicher and Fernando Reimers from Harvard University conducted a rapid survey between 18 and 27 March 2020, with 333 responses from 99 different countries. Bahçeşehir University was one of the collaborators of the survey. It clearly defined the current situation worldwide and the need of digitalization in education.

Digital Transformation means enhancing an organization's core operations to meet requirements efficiently by leveraging data and technology.

Top eight digital transformation trends in education are improved accessibility and access, personalized learning approaches, virtual reality, cloud-based learning opportunities, incorporating the internet of things into the school environment, security across digital devices, teaching digital citizenship, big data.

Paradigm Shift in Education

A paradigm shift is a radical change in the core concepts and practices of a given domain, discipline, or field. Paradigm shifts can occur at any of these levels and may cut across these levels. The field of education, at both the basic and higher education levels, has undergone tremendous change since COVID-19 pandemic.

Hybrid Teacher

Different platforms require different approaches. The future is in teachers who use learning methods effectively and create new methods on all platforms. The concept of "hybrid teacher" will now be a fact of our lives. Every teacher, due to their profession, can adapt very quickly to technology and changing educational environments. It does not matter whether a teacher is a generation of "digital natives" born into technology or a generation of "digital immigrants" who later got adapted into technology.

Another important concept that stands out with the concept of "Hybrid Teacher", is teachers' role as digital education leader. In this sense, it is important that we, as the education community, provide correct and sufficient materials in teacher training. We need to provide teachers with digital and pedagogical instruments in the light of new technologies. When this is done, we see that our teachers adapt very quickly to transformations and immediately begin to use these instruments to create new methods. The role of teachers in this process changes, but never loses its importance. In time, we see that teaching has ceased to be the source of the learning action. We observe that teaching essentially approaches the concept of mentor. This transformation will accelerate as all these technologies, and especially "Artificial Intelligence Technology", increase in education.

Hybrid / Blended Education

We can define "hybrid / blended education" as an education model that combines the advantages of digital education and traditional education. The most advanced form of distance education today can be expressed as digital education. The hybrid learning model is defined as the enrichment or blending of the traditional education method with online education materials. Traditional learning methods have been enriched with collaborative and technology-based education methods. In addition to the technologies used, the use of different educational philosophies in the traditional learning environment is also a part of this education model.

Historical Development of Distance Education

Distance education applications first started through letters. March 20, 1728, is a milestone for the development of distance education. On this date it was stated in the Boston Newspaper that "Shorthand Lessons" would be carried out through distance education. In an advertisement dated back to 1833, it was clearly stated that education would be carried out through letters. The rapid change in mass media has changed the face of distance education studies. In United States back in the 1920s, universities started to establish their own radios and offered educational services to the masses.

In 1923, educational radio programs started and over 500 different radio stations started to serve for this purpose. By the 1930s, the radio began to be used all over the world and educational programs gained momentum. The public was informed about subjects such as transportation, science, and technology through radio programs. Likewise, the broadcasts reached almost 1 million students and thus distance education applications were preferred through radio broadcasts. (Çoban, 2013)

Japan is among the countries that give importance to distance education. Within the scope of the 1948 lean education law, distance education applications started to teach soldiers, those who could not attend schools or those who were far from schools. In this framework, all students were provided with the opportunity to receive education at secondary, high school and higher education levels. The distance education model preferred by Japan was quite like that of the UK. Canada, tried to offer a comprehensive distance education service inspired by the United States. Distance education applications with a deep-rooted history in Canada are currently used all over the world. (Antalyalı, 2004)

The rapid change in mass media such as radio and television has enabled these channels to be used in the field of distance education as well. In 1972, the 'National University of Distance Education' was established by Spain. Large numbers of people benefit education opportunities. During this period, the foundations of today's distance education systems were laid in the developed countries of Europe. 'National College' was established in England in 1974 and then 'Hagen Open Education University' started to serve in Germany. (Uşun, 2016)

In Turkey, the first steps towards distance education were taken in 1927. Especially the physical deficiencies of educational institutions have enabled the development of distance education. This system has been actively used in primary, secondary, high school, and higher education degrees over time. On June 2, 1927, the Minister of National Education, Undersecretary, Members of National Education and Discipline, 11 Ministers of Education and the General Director came together and discussed the basic problems of education in Turkey. In this meeting, the education systems of developed countries were examined, and it was agreed that the solution to the education problem in Turkey would be the method of educating through mail. (Arar, 1999)

In the late 1950s and early 1960s, the contribution of letter-based education to education attracted high attention and as a result, a 'Teaching through Mailing Center' was established within the scope of the 'Statistical Publication Directorate'. Although it provides a one-dimensional and limited education opportunity, it clearly reveals the importance that Turkey has given to distance education. It expanded the scope of distance education in Turkey. The success of the center paved the way for the establishment of the 'Higher Teacher School', 'Correspondence Faculty', 'Correspondence High School', 'Correspondence Primary School and Broadcasting', and 'Broadcasted Higher Education Institution'. (Arar, 1999)

In 1968, the name of the 'Teaching through Mailing Center' was changed to the 'Radio and Television Education Center' by the high spread of radio and television. In 1982, the emergence of new educational technologies, The Radio and Television Education Center continued to serve as an 'Informatics Center'. In the 1980s distance education gained rapid momentum in Turkey. Since this period, was the renewal of the technological infrastructure which can meet the education needs of the people. (Papi & Büyükaslan, 2007)

The distance education model in higher education first started in Eskişehir Anadolu University 'Correspondence Faculty'. (Çukadar & Çelik, 2003)

Distance education, which started through a letter, has expanded its coverage area by making use of the internet infrastructure. In this way, people living in different countries and regions have started to use their right of receiving education. It is possible for students to gain more efficiency from the classroom environment since distance education programs that provide services both simultaneously and asynchronously can be carried out one-on-one. Distance education is widely used in developed and developing countries. It is possible to say that distance education will fill the deficiencies of formal education, which cannot be successful, especially due to physical and economic inconvenience. It has become possible to obtain diplomas in associate, undergraduate and graduate degrees through distance education. Distance education is also of great importance for Turkey. The lack of the desired level and quality of formal education has increased the value given to distance education. Since the high number of students reduces the efficiency in the classrooms, distance education can provide more beneficial results in terms of individual development and at the same time reinforce the transferred information with audio-visual examples. Internet-based distance education's use of new media tools and the use of computer infrastructure facilitated access to information and positively affected the desire of all segments of all ages to receive education. Distance education services, which have a deep-rooted history in Turkey, have provided an increase in individual success and formed the basis for higher quality preparation of independent studies. It is extremely important that distance education contributes to the right of every segment of every age to receive education by eliminating the time and space limits. (Ali Murat Kırık, 2014)

Hybrid / Blended Learning

It is recommended to combine traditional and online educational approaches as a solution to the limitations encountered in the use of traditional face-to-face learning and technology and internet-based approaches in the educational process alone. Thus, technology-based, and online educational activities can be combined as part of traditional learning environments in line with the needs of the student. (Rowley, Bunker, & Cole, 2002)

Definitions of Hybrid / Blended Learning

This new approach is defined in Turkish, mainly "blended learning" or "hybrid learning" however (Wilson & Smilanich, 2005) in the international literature "hybrid learning" (Tabor, 2007; Zitter & Hoove, 2012) or "mixed mode learning". (Huang, Lin, & Huang, 2012) It is 'an approach created by minimizing the disadvantages of face-to-face learning and online learning environments in the classroom and combining the advantageous aspects of these two learning environments' and 'learning systems that combine face-to-face instruction with computer-assisted instruction' as Graham declared. 'A method that combines various learning-teaching approaches with different information and communication technologies, offering the most appropriate learning environment for students regardless of time and place' as Bersin accepts.

Hybrid Learning Goals

Hybrid learning aims to combine the lessons taught face-to-face and online simultaneously. It is a type of blended learning that focuses on combining the physical classroom and digital learning spaces closer together into a more complete education. In the hybrid education model, students can have a combination of both face-to-face classes and digital learning. In such an education system model, while students attend classes at school two to three days a week; they continue the courses that follow the curriculum with digital education. Hybrid education is a customized learning opportunity for students who continue to be together with their teachers in face-to-face and digital classrooms in this process. One of the most advantageous aspects of hybrid education, when these arrangements are made effectively, the content and materials become more effective than traditional classroom education. The reason for this is that hybrid education equips the teaching process with more active learning applications such as case studies developed in digital environments, individual tests suitable for learning speed, and online group projects instead of the direct narration method that students receive in their classrooms. education is thought to be a successful model in the academic, social, and cognitive development of students. One of the most important advantages of hybrid education is that it reduces traffic in schools and enables more effective use of classroom spaces. Taking advantage of this advantage of hybrid education, especially during the pandemic process, can be seen as a situation that allows students, teachers, and the education process to be improved.

Digital Platforms

In digital education, a quality content and appropriate way of transfer are essential for the realization of student-centered, effective learning. And synchronous and asynchronous platforms are also very important. Perhaps the most important point in this crisis is the availability of access to online platforms for learning. The efficient use of digital tools and information technologies to improve teaching and learning also depends on the principles and practices of schools. (OECD 2020) PISA 2018 asked school administrators whether they had formal guidelines (written explanations, schedules, or guidelines, etc.) or practical implementations (regular meetings, etc.) focused on the efficient use of digital classrooms. Across OECD countries, the most common school practices targeted to reinforce learning within the use of digital tools are as follows: regular meetings between school management and teachers about digital tools used for pedagogical purposes (63 % of students went to schools with this practice), use of digital tools (62 % of students) and specific programs that prepare students to engage in conscious internet behavior (60 % of students). On the contrary the least common school practices across OECD countries are as follows: specific practices that will contribute to teacher collaboration on the use of digital tools. It has been observed that school guidelines and practices that aim to improve teaching and learning using digital tools more widely in socio-economically advantageous schools than in disadvantaged schools.

Technology and Educational Technologies

According to Turkish Statistical Institute (Turkish Statistical Institute, 2020) Household Information Technologies Usage Survey 2020, Computer and Internet use was 59.6 % and 72.9 %, respectively, in individuals aged 16–74 in 2018. These rates were 56.6 % and 66.8 %, respectively, in 2017. Computer and Internet usage rates were 68.6 % and 80.4 % for men in the 16–74 age group, while it was 50.6 % and 65.5 % for women. Eight out of ten households have

Internet access. According to the results of the household information technologies usage survey, in April 2018, 83.8 % of the households had access to the Internet from home. This rate was 80.7 % in the same month of 2017. The rate of individuals using the Internet was 79.0 %. The rate of internet usage was 79.0 % in individuals aged 16–74 in 2020. This rate was 75.3 % the previous year. When the internet usage rate is analyzed by gender; this rate was 84.7 % for men and 73.3 % for women. It was observed that 90.7 % of the households had access to the Internet from home. This rate was 88.3 % in the previous year.

According to data provided by "Grand View Research" (Grand View Research, Inc. Technology, 2020), the educational technologies market is expected to reach $285.2 billion in 2027 with an annual growth of 18 %.

Investment in Educational Technologies 2018–2025 (billion dollars) (Statista Feb. 2019)

	2018	2025
Virtual Augmented Reality	1.8	12.6
Artificial Intelligence	0.8.	6.1
Robotics	1.3	3.1
Blockchain	0.1	0.6

Artificial Intelligence Technologies and Personal Education Model

McKinsey published a report on "How will Artificial Intelligence impact K-12 teachers in 2019?" (Bryant, C.H., Saurabh S., and Dilip W., 2020) which shows that between 20 and 40 % of teaching hours are spent on activities that can be automated using existing technologies. Current technological development can help teachers reallocate 20–40 % of their time to activities that support students learning. By this way they better mentor the student. Inspiring students, building positive school and classroom climates, resolving conflict, connecting, and belonging, seeing the world from the perspective of individual students, and taking time to mentor and coach students. Which we call "Personal Education Model". Learning will be more permanent and more fun as it appeals to many senses. When it is used in all areas where it is not possible to experience in the distance education process and even in the subjects that are difficult to experience after distance education, performing the activities in the virtual environment and observing the results will contribute to the learning process. Since students are actively involved in the learning process, their motivation for learning will increase and learning will take place in a time and space nondependent manner.

5 G Technology and VR/ AR/ MR/ Hologram Applications

5G technology, will provide easier access to virtual reality, augmented reality, mixed reality, and hologram technologies that will allow us to use many stimuli more effectively. These technologies are now hard-to-reach, expensive, and applied, although they do not work very well. However, it is possible to actively use and spread in education. Just like the smart board technology, which caused great excitement when it came out years ago and really facilitates many things in education, these technologies can become widespread with 5G.

Integrating technology into the classroom is key to equipping students for success, according to a new ICTC report. The report, which surveys technology's impact on education in Canada, tells us that artificial intelligence is changing the way students learn and can help those with difficulties such as anxiety or difficulty maintaining attention. Artificial intelligence and machine learning can be used to personalize curriculum based on students' progress and their individual interactions with different courses.

The experiences it can provide – such as virtually witnessing endangered plant species in Madagascar – can ultimately change the way students think, relate to the world, and tackle problems. A new study published in the journal "Nature Biotechnology", which found 76 % increase in learning outcomes when students used a VR simulation, and 101 % increase in learning outcomes when used in conjunction with traditional teaching. (Makransky,G., Andreasen, N.K., Baceviciute, S., & Mayer R.E., 2020); Director of policy and outreach, Information and Communications Technology Council, Nathan Snider, says AR and VR technologies are being used in innovative ways around the world, particularly in the European Union. "Previously, we had the luxury of discussing whether a blended learning environment or an e-learning environment would be valuable to students," he says. "We don't have that luxury anymore. COVID-19 has shown us that it's timeless to seize new opportunities and new ways of learning" says Snider. (ICTC, 2020)

Transforming Education

Here are some of the new educational tools and aspects we foresee and already experience.

Tactile Internet and Skill Set Communication

Having a network capable of transmitting haptic communication over the internet will assist us in transitioning from today's content and information distribution to manual skill set distribution. This will open new opportunities for Tele-teaching and Tele-mentoring, particularly for manual training and skill development. The use of the tactile Internet in education can give distance education and remote team building a new definition and experience. To have a natural haptic interaction of our limbs with video and audio feedback, the service's response time must be very low, i.e. a few milliseconds round trip time forecasted only by 5G.

Virtual Reality and Education

While the first usage of Virtual Reality is in the entertainment industry, it also has implementations in education and training, and will play an important role in providing quality education and fostering understanding-based learning among students. While the first usage of Virtual Reality is in the entertainment industry, it also has implementations in learning and skills, and will play an important role in providing quality education and fostering understanding-based learning among students. It can also provide new experiences for distance learning and allow students to participate virtually in the classroom. This type of service necessitates extremely high bandwidth (bidirectional) and extremely low latency (i.e., 2–4ms).

Augmented Reality and Education

AR, like virtual reality, has already begun to show its relevance and utility in education. By providing the necessary information, contextual learning can become ubiquitous and pervasive. AR can be a powerful tool for delivering the right amount of information to the right audience at the right time. Through services such as Virtual Presence, it can enable new ways of learning and teamwork in education. AR can be used for more than just improving the learning experience. It can also assist teachers in gathering the necessary information about each student and becoming aware of their unique needs and abilities. For the implementation of such services, requirements such as optimized routing, seamless wide-area coverage, virtual presence, low-latency speech, and video encoding must be considered.

Walled Classroom

By combining tactile internet and virtual reality, future experiences in teaching and learning can go far beyond what is currently available. This eliminates the physical location constraint for experimental applications, allowing them to be used in large numbers regardless of their current location. It can facilitate and enable students to share resources. The impact will be greater in hands-on experience with expensive equipment and facilities. Individual access to a mobile device has the potential to connect each student to intelligent personalized systems that can suggest learning paths, enable aggregated analytics, and enable far better decision-making about all aspects of student experiences through better data capture. Categorizing students into different groups and recommending different multimedia content can put a strain on the network.

Wireless Backpack

Cloud-based storage services now allow users to access files regardless of the device they are using. Even with a relatively fast internet connection, there is significant latency in accessing content due to cloud providers' centralized architecture. Using future mobile technology, distributed cloud, and mobile edge computing, you can access content from a single device from anywhere. To access their personal content and stored files, the user only requires a device. Students can use this feature to continue their studies at a convenient time and location using various devices, giving the impression of immediate response time.

Special Needs Student

Advances in mobile technology and robotics may open new avenues for assisting children with special needs and engaging learning more accessible to them. Cloud-based robots can serve as a full-time assistant for students with disabilities, assisting them in interacting with other students and the educational environment. Instead of contacting a teacher for assistance (which can waste both the student's and the teacher's productive time), they can resolve the issue with the assistance of their robot.

Iot and Smart Classroom / Smart Campus

From smart buildings to smart healthcare, IoT applications touch every aspect of our lives. However, one of the fastest growing areas of these applications is education, which can improve our teaching, learning, and campus operations today.

IoT applications can also help us change the role of teachers in the classroom by reducing administrative burdens and allowing them to focus on their students. Automatically entering the classroom as soon as you walk in, a signal to distract you if you lose concentration during class, real-time feedback to a lecturer on areas where students still have problems based on their real-time analysis, these are just a few examples of how IoT and connected classrooms can improve the learning and teaching experience.

Cone of Experience Model

The more you experience, the better you learn. One forgets what he hears, recalls what he sees, and learns what he does.

Conclusion

Core result of digital transformation in education during and after COVID-19 is improving the access to quality education of millions around the world. Reaching out girls, disadvantaged groups, and children with special educational needs, etc. Change offers and will keep on offering many opportunities through quality education which will improve the living conditions of millions of people. This solution will address the rising income inequalities and will reverse the decrease in global productivity.

Education is the only power that will make the world better than it is today, and it is vital for the whole world to seize every opportunity that opens for education.

Erdal Karahan

Chapter 7 Regulatory Actions in Finance and How it Can Help Adopting Esg Criteria

Introduction

Previous chapters of this book have offered some perspective about sociological, political and economic macro effects of "Great Reset", why it is needed and, to our understanding, why it is inevitable. Beginning from this chapter the focus will be on the financial regulation part of the reset. The reasoning in this chapter of the book is simple, regulating over real sector is a tedious and cumbersome task which requires too much attention to details and in the end not offering a performance criterion that is comparable among sectors, regions, and countries.

Finance sector on the other hand offers many chances and short cuts for a general steering of the whole economy towards a more environmental and social equality friendly direction. Regulating over finance sector based on some universal criteria is easier, effective, comparable, and probably less biased. The idea of sustainable finance and impact financing are two main paradigms that can help us articulate the advantages and the historical path to regulating the great reset through finance sector. Although it has seen a rapid coming-of-age in 2020, partly in response to the COVID-19 pandemic as well as ongoing sustainability concerns, the sustainable finance idea is not new to literature nor to policy makers. It has been quiet a time since many researchers and leaders of developed economies started to dwell on the idea of sustainable finance.

Concern of sustainability of economic activities and its adverse effects on environment and social structures have been discussed for decades, even centuries (Piketty, 2013; Ziolo et al., 2019; Vosloo, 2014). The debate is old and throughout the history had been visited a lot yet the linkage between finance and sustainability have never been studied as thoroughly as the last two decades. Although the idea of social capital and environmental capital are much older (Coleman, 1988; Solow, 1986 and Hartwick, 1990), Elkington (1998), was one of the pioneers that proposes a linkage between the three pillars[1] (environmental, societal and financial) in assessing the performance of companies. Similar to

1 Originally called "Triple Bottom Line" a phrase writer John Elkington have coined in 1994.

Elkington a number of different criteria have been proposed to quantify the performance of companies by considering all three pillars. Among them notable mentions are environmental, social and corporate governance (ESG) criteria in investment decision-making, socially responsible investing (SRI) or principles for responsible investment (PRI) approaches, the impact investing and the principles for positive impact finance along with principles for responsible banking.

The question regarding what kind of criteria that should be used is still not answered. However sustainable development goals (or Millennium development goals) announced by UN set a clear objective about what to strive for. United Nations Environment Program (UNEP) and World Bank's numerous sustainability and development projects have spearheaded for a transition towards a climate-neutral economy and a fairer society since 1970s. However not until recently major economies take an action to make the sustainability their center of attention. Two milestones are important in the widespread adoption of the sustainability in public eyes, United Nations Sustainable Development Goals (SDG[2]) and Paris Agreement in 2015.[3] SDG aims to mobilize efforts to end all forms of poverty, fight inequalities and tackle climate change, while ensuring that no country is left behind. Although not binding governments are expected to commit the goals and take necessary actions to achieve 17 goals listed in the UN-SDG Summit by 2030. The Paris Agreement on the other hand sets out a global framework to avoid dangerous climate change by limiting global warming to below 2°C above pre-industrial levels (and if possible continuing efforts to limit it to 1.5°C). It also aims to strengthen countries' ability to deal with the impacts of climate change and support them in their efforts (COP 21 2015). Its importance also lies on the fact that 191[4] out of 197 countries in the world has ratified the agreement and announced strong commitment to meet the requirements.

---

2 See Annex 7–1, for the Latest Report see The Sustainable Development Goals Report 2020.

3 Kyoto Protocol's importance and precedence to the Paris agreement, should also be noted here. With Kyoto Protocol an agreement in which there are binding targets and measures for combating climate change exist, is accepted by international community for the first time. It also stipulates global ceilings for greenhouse gas emissions. It operationalizes the United Nations Framework Convention on Climate Change by committing industrialized countries (and economies in transition) to limit and reduce greenhouse gases (GHG) emissions in accordance with agreed individual targets.

4 Countries that have not ratified the agreement yet are: "Iran, Turkey, Iraq, Yemen Libya and Eritrea.

In the next section a review of the discussion on externalities in economics literature along with ESG criteria and sustainable finance will be discussed. At section 3 sources of changes that are the main drivers behind the need for a new regulatory system and why it should prioritize to solve problems related with these changes will be explained. At the fourth section current regulatory actions and pressures will be explained along with some insights about how future regulatory actions should consider.

Externalities and ESG Criteria

The existence of externalities and how to solve it, is a widely investigated concept. Unregulated markets have a reluctance to price externalities, at least not at the right level, because often the party that produces the externality and carries the burden of it are different agents. Marshall's and Pigou's earlier works contain traces of the idea of externalities however in modern economics the debate for externalities is accepted to be introduced by Pigou (1920) with Pigouvian tax which can be described as a form of Polluter's Pay Principle. But before him through the Middle Ages the idea was widely accepted and historically the principle can be traced back to Plato.[5]

Starting from the early 20th century numerous researchers and policy makers have studied the different mechanisms behind the externalities. Externalities (irrespective of being good or bad) stemming from almost every economic and social activity (i.e. from severe poverty's impact on growth to the tragedy of commons) have been investigated during this period in order to better understand them and come up with the socially optimal methods to manage them. In theory externalities doesn't always have to be bad, in some cases they can be desirable and society might want to be subject to such externalities even more than the current amount (e.g. positive externalities due to education and health-care or spill-over effects of technology companies). Buchanan and Stubblebine (1962) present a mathematical representation of externalities in which externality is an independent variable of the welfare function of an economic entity. In their representation if an economic welfare task is affected by other factors not controlled by itself, it is defined as an externality and its nature doesn't have to be negative or positive. Marshall (1922), Pigou (1920) and Coase (1960) were among the first ones that define the externalities from the point of view of sustainable

5 *"If anyone intentionally spoils the water of another ... let him not only pay damages, but purify the stream or cistern which contains the water..."* – Plato

development and each formulated their own method of solution for reaching a socially desirable solution. While Pigou advocates state intervention (e.g., taxes) as a solution, Coase showed that negative externalities can be eliminated not only through instruments like taxes but also through institutional solutions (like property rights).

One thing important to note here is the understanding of the nature of the externality is key to success in dealing with it. Although government intervention may present a Pareto optimal outcome it may not be desirable for the economic agents. The opposite is also true although economic agents may reach a desirable outcome within themselves the result may not be Pareto optimal or sustainable due to lack of inter-generational representation in the problem. Therefore, clear determination of goals and quantification of the impact of externalities due to absence of them, are very important when battling with social and environmental injustice.

While externalities resulting from industrial and agricultural activities can be calculated with relative ease due to traceability of inputs used in the production processes, externalities stemming from service sector are much harder to calculate since it is usually a combination of different factors, and the marginal effect of each factor may not be calculated since combinations of some externalities may result higher or lower costs than their individual effect. Moreover, cost of externalities due to socially undesirable problems like gender or income inequalities are almost impossible to calculate at micro level. Externalities resulted from the activities of companies in finance sector is even harder to track. Apart from financing some individual projects it is quite hard to pinpoint the impact of credits and general financial services on environment and society since direct link between them and firm's activities is almost impossible to establish.

Sustainable Finance a term coined to overcome this missing link is becoming more and more center of focus for the past two decades. Unfortunately, there are too many definitions of sustainable finance out in the market. Furthermore, both private and public institutions tend to create their own definition or shape the existing ones such that it is aligned with their institutional goal. Migliorelli (2021) addresses the problem and tries to come up with an inclusive definition while also stating that it is not an easy task. Although this chapter's main objective is not to define "the" description of sustainable finance it is crucial to create an all-inclusive description such that a criteria to assess economic actors' performance in meeting these goals can be uniformly measured, in order to reach the aforementioned unbiased, effective and comparable policy tools. Creation of that kind of criteria can also prevent the concerns about greenwashing or sustainable washing (Dahl, 2010) and will prevent abuse of eco-friendly term by the market.

Pillar	Thomson Reuters	MSCI	Bloomberg
Environmental	Resource Use Emissions Innovation	Climate Change Natural resources Pollution & waste Environmental opportunities	Carbon Emissions Climate change effects Pollution Waste disposal Renewable energy Resource depletion
Social	Workforce Human Rights Community Product Responsibility	Human capital Product liability Stakeholder opposition Social opportunities	Supply chain Discrimination Political contributions Diversity Human rights Community relations
Governance	Management Shareholders CSR strategy	Corporate governance Corporate behaviour	Cumulative voting Executive compensation Shareholders' rights Takeover defence Staggered boards Independent directors
Key metrics and submetrics	186	34	>120

Figure 7.1: ESG Criteria
Source: Boffo and Patalano – 2020 – ESG Investing Practices.

Among many alternatives ESG indices seem to be the closest thing that can offer such a common criteria. Index scoring usually starts with determination of which drivers to be included under each pillar of E, S and G. this is followed by independent (or in some cases co-dependent) assessment of each driver and as the last step weighing and creating the final ESG score. There is a wide range of rating practices in terms of determining which data to include and how to weigh metrics while calculating the ESG scores. This is expected when different priorities among industries and countries are considered. What is not expected is similar companies or industries being evaluated differently in terms of their ESG performance by different rating providers. Common ESG criteria of major index providers are presented in Figure 7.1.

Alternatives to the ESG score that can be used for assessing the performance of policies implemented to achieve sustainability can be SRI (or PRI) based scoring or using Impact financing practices as a tool to help implementation of sustainability related goals. Both methods employ similar tools with some differences about what should be primary and secondary goals or how to achieve them though, the general approach is similar. It consists of determination of which activities, actions and sectors are relevant to the company's business type than defining the impact of each driver which can be either negative positive or neutral. And in the final step achieving a final impact score based on weights and adopted impact score methodology.

The methodology might be singular or twofold depending on the business or the region of the company under evaluation. If the company in question is a financial institution or a very big corporation that is doing business with too many small companies or own many affiliates than these third parties should also be included in the impact calculation. In fact, inclusion of third parties' impact might be included in any case to reach a holistic assessment. However, this might be impractical for small firms due to their capabilities to do such estimations.

For determination of negative, neutral and positive impacts there are published exclusion lists, safeguard policies and certification systems. As well as UNEP's tools to calculate impact for different sectors and business types. UNEP-FI (2019, 2017) also offers an extensive approach to calculate impact for Banks and other financial institutions. One thing to note here is that each sector has its own dynamics and the same impact score for different sectors does not mean that both companies are equally successful at battling with inequality and environmental problems. Some sectors are inherently more eco-friendly than others (i.e., organic farming vs steel industry) thus when impact scoring is adopted to be used, institutions should be aware of that and classify businesses based on their peers' performances or against the benchmark objective of that sector. The list can be altered by adding the concerns regarding climate change, human rights, marine life perseverance, eco-diversity or any of such topics at the center or the periphery of the assessment criteria.

Increased commitment to the sustainability goals by governments and the rise of average person's interest to the sustainability in the last two decade is not a product of activists and researchers alone. Current outlook in terms of economic, social, and environmental well-being of world is the main driver behind it. Sadly, the last two decades have witnessed unprecedented change in the degradation of environmental and social capital. In the next section, drivers behind this degradation will be explained in more detail along with its likely evolution during the 21st century unless decisive actions are taken to heal it.

Sources of Changes in Economic and Social Life

Signs of radical and lasting changes in our economic and sociological system has begun to appear for at least a decade. The global economic crisis of 2008 has marked the beginning of widespread questioning of the market mechanism and its inability to solve crisis by itself originally raised in late 70s and early

80s (Georgescu – Roegen, 1975; Stiglitz, 1989). The trends that were persistent throughout the last three decades and forces us to review our understanding on the relationship between economy and society were increased robotization and automation in the production and decreasing income equality through most of the developed and developing countries. These two trends might also be held responsible for the great reset this book has focused on, and unfortunately, they are very unlikely to disappear.

A third source of change has made itself very apparent during this period as well, Environmental Degradation. Now we realize that Earth is not infinite, and we are merely tenants not the proprietor of it. Understanding this reality was the final piece of the puzzle that changes the paradigm. As Jeucken (2001) states it, once a prevailing paradigm is not sufficient to find answers for the questions raised a new paradigm develops to answer them. It is a new way of thinking about old as well as new problems and old concepts are replaced with new ones or at least re-identified by the new paradigm.

Since 2008 more and more researchers and policy makers are accepting the new paradigm and trying to formulate some solutions within it. On the one hand it is imperative to employ regulations to slow down and (possibly) recover from the environmental and social degradation, on the other hand we have yet to define the actual impacts, uniform quantification tools for SDG drivers and cost of it. Almost every report, research, or analysis on cost of meeting SDG criteria tries to present a definitive number for it. Although not conclusive these estimations implies a range from USD 5–7 Trillion (OECD, 2017[b]) annually. Considering that these estimations possibly neglect the interdependencies, inefficiencies, and any kind of spillover effects it is hard to place reliance on them while estimating costs and benefits of such a healing process.

That is why in this chapter it is argued that incentives on finance sector through regulations can do the trick with less intervention and more efficiency. Although it requires a careful classification and quantification of economic activities and labor force committed by each economic agent and their likely trends for the foreseeable future it enables policy – makers to incentivize economic agents based on their performance on selected criteria.[6] Therefore it is important

6 Throughout this chapter SDG criteria will be referred since we have some idea about cost and completion of them due to UNEP and other institutions' reports. However, the author does not argue that SDG criteria fit in completely to the idea of Great Reset which is more general and contains improvements in income, wealth, and other social inequalities on top of SDG criteria.

to know the sources of changes in each sector for a better understanding of the responsibilities of institutions in each sector (both public and private) and what kind of risks they might face in the upcoming decades for a sustainable economy. From a regulatory viewpoint it is also important to know what type of problems the industry is likely to face soon to be able to decide what kind of regulatory practices will be desirable to implement. This chapter classifies the risks under three group: technological, sociological and environmental. For the rest of this section, we will have a quick look on the sources of changes and associated risks in financial sector.

Sources of Change: Technological

Although not completely dominated the existing production methods yet, this past decade we have been experiencing an unstoppable rise of AI based automated services. This process can be traced back to 90's in which world economy met with an increase in efficiency due to widespread integration of computers and web-based services at workplace. This period even had its own little-crisis called "*dot-com bubble*". Although at that time collapse of communism and integration of both Eastern Block and China to global economy draw much more attention than the subtle (yet unavoidable) transition to this new type of production method most people realized that a new type of industrial revolution was on the way (Autor et al., 1998).

We are at a technological level that we can be sure that most of the jobs will continue to be automatized in the future and workers will need to adjust their skill set and jobs. What we are not sure is the total effect of it. Will it increase or decrease the available jobs and if so for whom? One likely result of automatization is, it can exacerbate economic inequalities by decreasing the available jobs for middle skilled workers while increasing the low and high skilled jobs (OECD, 2017[a]) which may increase income inequality even more.

Before they made their way into our day-to-day business and social life, information technologies and artificial Intelligence, was still growing in different forms but mostly as a type of consumer good. What is important within the scope of this chapter is the impact they have when they start to replace old production methods in several industries. Very similar to its predecessors (like steam power and electricity) this new revolution of industry not just brought new types of goods or methods to produce them it also has changed the dynamics of our society and composition of its workforce and relationship between them.

For a better understanding of the changes, it presents let's start with its effect on the overall economy before passing to the effects on the Banks and

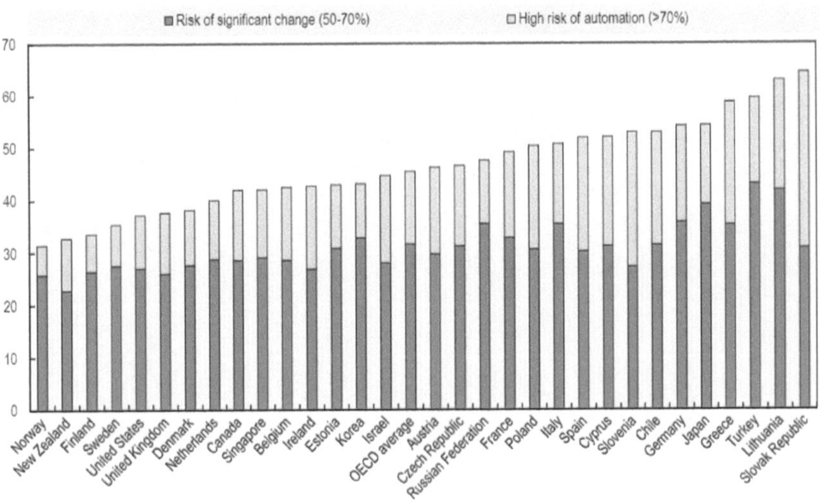

Figure 7.2: Job Polarization by Country
Source: OECD Employment Outlook 2017.

financial sector. Increased automation in production have already started (and may be almost finished) to replace labor workforce in the manufacturing sector. However, its impact is not homogenous and not limited to the manufacturing jobs, in fact many studies have repeatedly shown that low skilled jobs are the ones that have been and will be affected most (Greenhalg et al., 2001; Bogliacino et al., 2011). A number of studies show that automation will replace large proportion of jobs in the future (Frey & Osborne, 2013; McKinsey Global Institute, 2017; Frey et al., 2016) and transforms other. Frey and Osborne 2013 also show that both skilled and unskilled labor will be affected from the automatization while unskilled physical labor is at the greatest risk, a finding that has been ratified by a wide range of studies afterwards. Figure 7.4 presents the PIAAC's survey of adult skills and jobs under risk of automation in OECD countries retrieved from Nedelkoska, L. and G. Quintini (2018)

Today world is talking about dark-factories in which human labor is only used for maintenance and second-level quality control processes. Building and operating such factories was a science fiction topic in the past or only attainable through huge investments and still the profitability of the process would be questionable. The improvements in artificial intelligence (AI) on the other hand made this a possibility (Ford, 2015). The amount of tasks AI made possible is

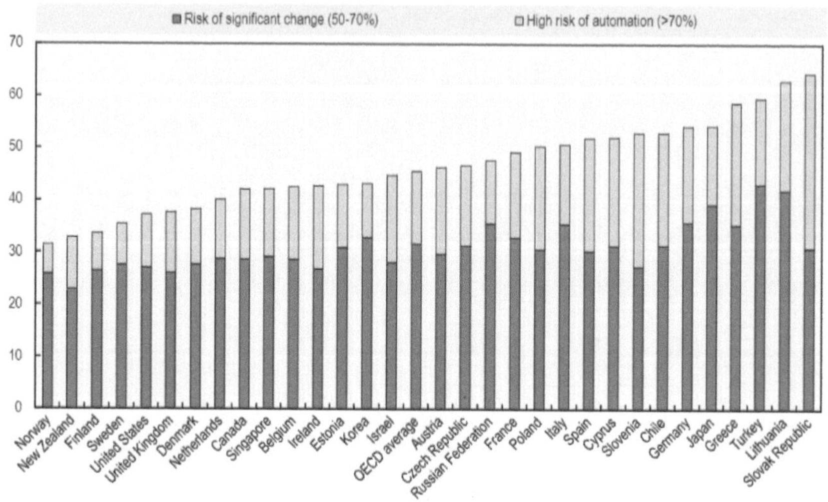

Figure 7.3: Jobs at Risk in OECD Countries

Source: OECD Social, Employment and Migration Working Papers, OECD 2018[b], Survey of Adult Skills (PIAAC) 2012.

not limited with the manufacturing sector. It is employed by most companies with great success not just in the production process also in the decision-making process. Therefore, automatization is now penetrating to the service sector and replacing manual labor with a great pace causing shifts and challenges in the labor markets.

Not all predictions are pessimistic though. Contradictory to the above studies a couple of studies have shown that rising automatization does not necessarily increase unemployment (Lane & Saint-Martin, 2021). The OECD 2021 report shows that 14 % of jobs are at high risk of automation but, even if the risk of automation is real employment grew in all OECD countries over the period 2012–2019. McKinsey Global Institute 2017 also show that even though automatization may displace almost 15 % of workforce it will probably create new jobs through the process. Some other studies have shown that automation might help creation of new jobs (Acemoglu & Restrepo, 2019; Artuc et al., 2018) due to its positive effect on flexible allocation of labor to the newly created tasks or further reductions in robot prices.

The overall effect on the income level and job stability is still debatable. Outcome of this process will probably be dependent on two things. First one is

Table 7.1: Technology's effect on finance sector

Technology's Overall Effect on Economy[1]	**Technology Effects on Banking & Finance Sector[2]**
• An increase in the unemployment rate which is very likely to be accompanied by an increase in inequality and a change in income. Overall lower income in middle class or high rate of unemployment will also affect the demand on companies' products	• Alternative organizations emerging as a competitor to traditional financial institutions, i.e. Fintechs, Within holding finance, Customer Financing Companies
• A higher rate of non-performing loans Degradation of portfolio quality	Increased competition and regulative pressure
• A lower rate of loan demand or acceptance rate for loan The effect on savings and deposit	• Use of Big-data and AI in finance sector Real time Decision Making and risk monitoring In-House vs Vendor Models,
• Re-education of existing workforce in order to make them compatible with new production methods	• Workforce Re-education

Source: Author's own deductions.

whether introduction of AI and increased automatization will create more job than they destroy. The second one is whether the nature of these new jobs will cause polarization between low skilled and high skilled jobs while destroying the middle-skilled jobs in the process or not. OECD 2017[a] shows that Job polarization by country has been increased between 1995 and 2015, while PIAAC's surveys continue to show that for the upcoming decades low-skilled jobs are at greater risk. Additionally, some economists argue that automation is more likely to increase productivity of capital does not labor thus might cause increasing income inequality (Mckay et al., 2019).

Based on the trends shared by OECD and UN and other independent researchers' studies, it can be argued that the picture will be very similar for workforce and automatization trends in Banking & Finance sector as well. For a better understanding of technologies' impacts it is better to categorize it under two topics. Its direct effects through labor market, automatization of tasks and adoption of AI and ML based solutions in the workstyle of these institutions and its indirect effects on customer/credit portfolio due to changing composition of income and employment statistics. Table 7.1 summarizes such impacts at below.

Sources of Change: Sociological

Increasing income inequality and concentration of wealth at the hands of upper classes have been a widely discussed topic in the literature. The literature goes as early as to 18th century (Piketty, 2013) however Kuznets (1955) should be given credit since he was the first one to note the decreasing trend in income inequality in US, a phenomenon that is also observed for other developed economies. Even though share of income and wealth of upper classes seem to decline through the 20th century's first two quarter Piketty (2013) argues that this decline was probably a consequence of political and sociological environment rather than the famous rising tides and the boat argument. His work and several others (Atkinson et al. 2011; Alvaredo et al. 2013) also shows the decreasing gap between upper and lower classes changes behavior during the last quarter of 20th century and ever since then it has been replaced by an increasing gap.

Piketty (2013) argues that economic growth will slow down and the rate of return to capital will exceed overall growth therefore he concludes that the growing capital share of income is likely to endure. Rising inequality trend can be seen in his works or many other researchers' works in the last decade (see World Social Report, 2020). One important thing to note about income inequality is, it might increase within a country while decreasing in general for the whole world. Data till 1980 shows that worldwide income inequality is decreasing mostly because high growth in Asian Countries (special thanks to China and India). On the other hand, within country inequality is rising sharply while middle income groups are squeezed in most of the western countries (World Inequality Lab, 2017). World Inequality database's latest findings on income inequality presented in World Social Report (2020) is presented below to give some idea.

About increasing gap in income inequality (and inequality of wealth distribution) most researchers argue that lower taxes for rich enabled them to save and invest more while imposing the tax burden to the backs of the low –income individuals. Proponents of tax cuts for rich usually put forward the famous "trickle-down" argument which basically claims that targeted tax cuts for rich is very likely to stimulate business investment in the short term and benefit society at large in the long term. While some cross-country empirical studies find that progressive taxation adversely affect economic growth (Gemmell et al., 2014; Padovano & Galli, 2002), a number of studies find no significant association (Angelopoulos et al., 2007; Hope & Limberg, 2020; Piketty et al., 2014) and some other studies show the opposite (Zidar, 2015).Whatever the reason is, the increasing gap in income does not just create low purchasing power for lower income classes unfortunately it also creates inequality of opportunities (Stiglitz, 2016).

	Africa	Asia	Latin America and the Caribbean	Europe, Northern America, Oceania and Japan	Total	Percentage of countries	Percentage of total population
Rising inequality							
1990-2016	13	9	1	26	49	41.2	71
1990-1999	n.a.	7	12	4	23		
2000-2007	n.a.	7	2	13	22		
2008-2016	n.a.	4	1	14	19		
Falling Inequality							
1990-2016	16	12	17	13	58	48.7	20.8
1990-1999	n.a.	2	4	4	10		
2000-2007	n.a.	8	13	13	34		
2008-2016	n.a.	13	13	14	40		
No trend							
1990-2016	2	3	1	6	12	10.1	8.2
1990-1999	n.a.	3	2	4	9		
2000-2007	n.a.	0	3	9	12		
2008-2016	n.a.	0	4	14	18		
Total	**31**	**24**	**19**	**45**	**119**		

Figure 7.4: Changing Income Inequality a Summary

Source: World Social report 2020, calculations are based on World Inequality Database. Available from: https://wid.world/data/.

The problem becomes more severe when cross –country differences are added. Inequality in developed countries is a matter of justice while inequality in developing or under-developed countries is a matter of life and death. Latest WSR report (2020) shows that unequal opportunities are affecting the unlucky groups more severely in low-income countries than the others. Unfortunately, rising income inequality is not the only source of inequality of opportunities. There seem to be several barriers that prevent the trickle down of the creation of opportunities as well. Several research have showed that members of ethnic minorities and other disadvantaged groups (gender, disability status, migrant origin, and parental socioeconomic status) are also more likely to remain in poverty over the long term. Immigration, climate change, technology and urbanization are stated as the other sources for income inequalities and biggest contributors of why it persists among different groups. The main reason for persistence of inequalities however seems to be barriers to access education and finance and imbalance between the bargaining powers of stakeholders (shareholders vs rest of the society).

The role and responsibility of financial institutions in the deterioration in income distribution and its correction is crucial here. Since 1970s both World

Bank and United Nations are actively trying to find solutions to alleviate the results of the problem, but a lasting solution has yet to present itself. Although the current picture is not very colorful the future is not so dim. The last couple of decades have witnessed changes in both consumers' behavior and shareholders' approach to capitalism. Relationship between ESG criteria and Corporate Financial Performance (CFP) has been studied extensively Friede et al. 2015, conducts an extensive literature research and shows that overall, the relationship between the two is non-negative whereas some other work (both earlier and later studies than Friede et al.) are showing negative correlation. Another common finding of the literature is that better ESG criteria often leads to better expectations for CFP and causing higher demand and subsequent overvaluation of the stocks. Moreover, higher demand for better ESG performers is not always fueled with better CFP expectations, data from Merrill lynch shows that 77 % of ESG investing is due to social or moral considerations (Boffo & Patalano, 2020). Although literature studying the link between ESG criteria and corporate performance is conflicting and a clear relationship is yet to be found, more and more investors are starting to prioritize ESG criteria (Boffo & Patalano, 2020).

Sources of Change: Ecological

In its essence the issue about natural resources can be summarized as good management of renewable and recyclable resources. To this end being aware of the relationship between ecology and economics is crucial. The later cannot exist without the former yet the vice versa is not true. Although some cultures realized this and treat environment with respect (Native Americans, Bushman of Africa and Aboriginals of Australia) modern society seems to have neglected this for a very long time and is now facing the consequences. "Tragedy of commons" a term coined by Hardin (1968),[7] illustrates the dilemma currently faced by society with ease and precision, on the one hand all economic agents are aware that overuse (or misuse) of natural resources will lead to inevitable depletion of them. On the other hand, they are also aware that their lower consumption will only enable other agents to consume more while not changing the result of depletion.

The club of Rome's 1972 report (Meadows et al.) was one of the earliest and most notable study claiming that Earth's resources and ecological system cannot support the current rates of economic and population growth beyond the 21st

7 Actually, the issue was first handled by Willian Forster Lloyd in 1833, in his "Two Lectures on the Checks to Population.

century. Although their model is criticized by some economists for being too simplistic and very sensitive to parameter variations it paved the way for further studies and deeper discussions. Today UNEP and United Nations Framework Convention on Climate Change (UNFCCC) are actively working to battle Environmental problems and meet annually since 1995 to determine new goals and assess the progress. In fact, famous Paris Agreement is a result of one of those meetings (COP 21). Unfortunately, climate change is not the only ecological problem that we should be worrying, the list is long and contains many challenges that are not less important than climate change. Steffen et al. (2015) defines a safe operating space for human societies to develop and thrive, based on the biophysical processes that regulate the Earth's ecosystem. They characterize safe- uncertain and high-risk zones for nine productive ecological capacities It can be observed that ecological capacities of climate change, land-system change (deforestation and land erosion), biodiversity loss (terrestrial /marine, genetic diversity) and biochemical flows (nitrogen and phosphorus, mainly because of intensive agricultural practices) have been crossed. For some ecological capacities (ozone depletion, ocean acidification and freshwater use) the risks are minimal or decreasing while for some others they were unable to define a boundary level (Novel entities and Aerosol loading).

Financial Institutions' responsibilities in battling with degradation of ecology can be grouped under two topics. The first one is assessing the risks related to the ecological problems and pricing the sustainability related risks. An example might be companies that are operating under high risk of hurricanes or farmers who work on land susceptible to erosion and salinization. On the one hand, the pricing of risks may result in an increase in the cost of accessing financial services for economic agents and ultimately cause a market failure since no financial institution will be willing to finance economic activities or insure the economic risks in high-risk environments. In such environments, interventions such as price control or cost support for the access to key financial services, promotion of ad hoc reinsurance schemes, more favorable fiscal treatment for stranded assets may also become necessary (Migliorelli & Dessertine, 2019).

The second one is financing sustainability related projects or adopting positive impact finance principles. UNEP-FI (2017) defines positive impact Finance as.

> *"It is that which serves to deliver a positive contribution to one or more of the three pillars of sustainable development (economic, environmental and social), once any potential negative impacts to any of the pillars have been duly identified and mitigated."*

It is true that Financial Institutions decisions can be influential since they can refuse to finance and service risks associated with certain sectors or types of

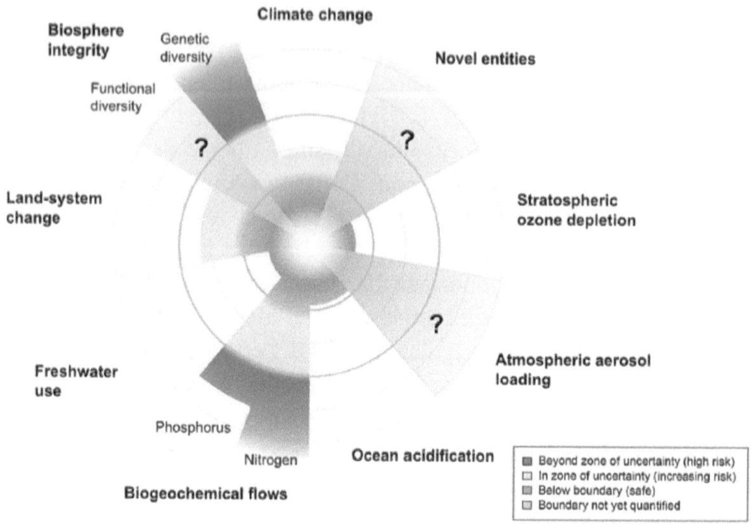

Figure 7.5: Ecological Capacities for Human Society
Source: Steffen et al., 2015.

operation. By increasing business costs or by requiring higher premiums for environmentally risky activities and products they can send signals to the investors, governments and all relevant stakeholders which can change the common view of what is risky and ultimately shape behaviors of economic agents (Bouma et al., 2017).

Regulatory Actions & Pressures

The driving forces of the change in financial sector explained at previous sections will inevitably trigger the management practices and stakeholders of the sector. In fact, significant events and shifts in geopolitics, global health, political elections, and climate change have already been transforming behaviors in the financial markets. The idea of sustainable finance, an idea which initially was adopted by just a small part of the banking sector for a long time, is moving to the center of attention each day. As it moves to the center of attention management practices and actions of financial institutions are also scrutinized more deliberately.

One of the reasons for the increased focus in the finance sector can be traced back to the 2008 crisis and institutions' lack of ability to foresee and prevent it. Before that we often see a huge but misplaced trust to market mechanism and its ability to calculate and price risks in the literature. Likewise, there was a widespread belief about markets, eventually pricing the risks related to environmental and social problems. Unfortunately, market pricing mechanism did not work then and will continue not working just because a very simple reason, externalities.

So, what is the solution? Society or in a more relevant sense policy makers must name the risks, price them, quota them and if necessary, enforce the socially desirable levels through different mechanisms. Even in the absence of clearly defined links between financial services and environmental and social externalities general ESG scores of company's sectors or economic activities can be used to develop optimum financing strategies. In practice we are already taking a diverse set of actions for most of the risks in financial sector. Establishment of first central banks and probably adoption of Keynes' idea and New Deal of President Roosevelt might be the earliest examples of such interventions by governments and regulators to the market. Today, widespread risk management practices are enforced by national and supranational regulatory bodies throughout the world to prevent financial crisis. Such an initiative could be employed to reach an everlasting solution for the threat to sustainable development.

As expected, the policy makers and regulatory bodies of national and international institutions are also reacting to the increasing frequency of environmental related crisis and social disturbances that have been experienced for the last two decades. As mentioned, previous chapters of this paper United Nations, World Bank, OECD are the biggest contributors to the issue not just by setting goals for sustainable development but also by actively monitoring the latest trends. Lately governments are starting to commit Sustainable Development Goals either through individual action plans or by adhering the international agreements and goals set by supra-national levels. Paris Agreement is one of these international agreements. It draws a broader picture for the signatory countries and leaves the design and specifics of action plans of each country to herself. The agreement is most famous for its goal to keep global warming below 2°C above the pre-industrial levels. But it also put great emphasis on Sustainable Development Goals and regulating finance flows such that low green-house-gas emissions and climate resilient development is ensured.

Since the idea of Great Reset and rethinking of global society is parallel to the goals set by SDG considering both objectives together help us to build analogies between the costs of reaching such objectives. Although Great Reset idea is focused on reshaping and redefining the existing relationships between the economic agents just like SDG, it is based on the unavoidable problems and constraints caused by environmental, technological, and social factors. Thus, having an idea about state of progress in reaching SDG also presents possible roadmaps and their cost for Great Reset. OECD estimates (from OECD, 2017[b] and OECD, 2018[a]) indicate that around USD 6.3 trillion of infrastructure investment is needed each year up until 2030 to reach sustainable development goals, and this investment need must increase to USD 6.9 trillion a year to make it compatible with the goals of the Paris Agreement. Reports on investment needs to attain SDG usually implies an investment need around USD 5–7 trillion annually (UNEP-FI, 2018). Latest World Investment Report (UNCTAD – WIR, 2020) informs that investment gap to reach SDG is around USD 2.5 trillion annually. An earlier study by (UNEP-FI, 2018) shows that only USD 0.1 trillion of this gap belongs to developed countries whereas almost all of it belongs to EMDEs (half of which is specifically for Africa). Reports also show that although green finance and ESG focused investing practices are growing the share of both activities are still below 1 % of the global size of their respective markets. These statistics indicate that such practices are still far away from being the mainstream financing activities and there is significant room to grow.

Within that respect it can be said that global community is far from reaching the SDG objectives and to reach those objectives adoption of more financial regulations regarding climate change and social development should be encouraged. Up until now endeavors to implement the idea of sustainable economic activities have been presented in the form of action plans and in a more voluntary way mainly focusing on incentive and reward schemes.[8] However, with more robust targets appearing in the agendas of governments and international institutions, new steps are more likely to include coercive actions. Before such actions to be taken, a set of criteria has to be chosen in order to establish standards to be followed. European Union's 2018 Commission Action Plan for Financing Sustainable Activities[9] is one of them. The action plan draws a very good outline for the future of possible regulatory practices within EU and other developed economies. The headline of the plan is shared at below table. It is grouped under three main topics which in total contain 10 key objectives.

As can be seen from the table, currently the action plan is mainly focused on describing and linking the environmental risks and economical activities rather than setting clear regulations for the finance sector through an accord. The action plan's priority set is also aligned with the expectation of the SDG but more

8 Carbon taxes implemented in developed economies can be exempt from this.
9 European Commission, 2018.

Table 7.2: EBA's sustainable finance activities

1. *Reorienting capital flows towards a more sustainable economy*
1. Establishing a clear and detailed EU taxonomy, a classification system for sustainable activities
2. Creating an EU Green Bond Standard and labels for green financial products
3. Fostering investment in sustainable projects
4. Incorporating sustainability in financial advice
5. Developing sustainability benchmarks
2. *Mainstreaming sustainability into risk management*
6. Better integrating sustainability in ratings and market research
7. Clarifying asset managers' and institutional investors' duties regarding sustainability
8. Introducing a "green supporting factor" in the EU prudential rules for banks and insurance companies
3. *Fostering transparency and long-termism*
9. Strengthening sustainability disclosure and accounting rule-making
10. Fostering sustainable corporate governance and attenuating short-termism in capital markets

importantly it paves the road for integration of Responsible Banking Criteria and regulatory standards by.

- Asking European financial institutions actively participate in sustainable finance practices
- Asking for sustainability related accounting rules, risk rating assessments and disclosures

Therefore, it would not be surprising to see good old financial regulations being expanded to include sustainability and environmental risks as important pillars. Moreover, it is very likely to see the future variants of Basel Accord including environmental and social criteria and rules for financial institutions as one of its pillars even if the level of global readiness is not sufficient.

Considering possible trends in the responsible investing framework and effort to meet ESG criteria the biggest challenge for finance sector in the upcoming years seems to be the need to comply with regulatory requirements and social objectives while maintaining the economic profitability. Schoenmaker (2017) defines three stages of sustainable finance (and one business as usual stage) to illustrate the relationship between varying degrees of integration of sustainable finance to the core strategy of the financial institution (from corporate philanthropy to the full integration). The stages move from finance only, to finance

Table 7.3: 3 Stages of sustainable finance by Schoenmaker

Sustainable Finance Typology	Value Created	Ranking of Factors	Optimisation	Horizon
Finance-as-usual	Shareholder value	F	Max F	Short term
Sustainable Finance 1.0	Refined Shareholder value	F > 5 and E	Max F subject to S and E	Short term
Sustainable Finance 2.0	Stakeholder value	T=F+S+E	Optimise T	Medium term
Sustainable Finance 3.0	Common good value	S and E > F	Optimise S and E subject to F	Long term

Note: F = financial value; S = social impact; E = environmental impact; T = total value. At Sustainable Finance 1.0, the maximisation of F is subject to minor S and F constraints.
Source: Schoenmaker 2017, A Framework for Sustainable Finance.

first (SF1.0), then to all aspects equal (SF2.0), and finally to social-environmental impact first (SF3.0). His analysis assumes of sustainability being crucial to corporate survival. This assumption might be oversimplifying without a clear coercion of regulatory body since in the absence of any kind of regulation or institutional control there is nothing preventing a company to commit free-riding and follow the temptation of maximizing financial revenue instead of common good.

Parallel to the needs of EBA's financial sustainability action plan (and SDG commitments) the accounting profession should also integrate pollution charges and clean-up costs and other ESG related investments and their stock and flow values to the balance sheets of companies. Such initiatives would make it easier for financial institutions to make operational decisions (Bouma et al., 2017). This integration should not just cover the realized clean –up costs or fines to be faced due to activities, it should be comprehensive and be able to attach monetary values to environmental, technological, and social risks. In terms of environmental risks there are diverse methods of calculation[10] however for technological and social risk attaching a monetary value might be challenging.

10 Such as; actuarial techniques, professional judgement and valuation methods, engineering cost estimates, decision making analysis techniques, modelling; scenario techniques, etc.

Current state of completion of SDG goals and reports discussing the future trends imply that the gap between financing needs to reach them and actual financing level is likely to increase in the future. To tackle increasing caps three alternatives present themselves. First one is private financial institutions will have to implement both environmental & social sustainability policies by takin initiatives themselves. They might choose to do so to gain access to already – established sustainable finance related private or public funds. Since this is the current method than the problem boils down to increase the size of such funds. Second alternative is, governments will have to make such investment by themselves. Although governments can do such investments this usually means that it must be done in expense of other public services or a fiscal expansion. Repercussions of governments' assuming that role is out of scope of this paper but in theory they can increase the current regulative actions to reach a Pigouvian type solution. And finally, the third alternative is a mixture of the two, change the taxation scheme such that it gives incentives to the ESG friendly actions in finance sector and penalizes the non-friendly ones. Widespread use of such an incentive scheme in finance sector will increase the funds available for environmental and social goals. Then the problem becomes what kind of incentive schemes should be preferred and under which conditions socially responsible financing practices can be adopted widely by private sector.

Some Insights for a New Regulatory System

Faced with regulatory pressures, general attitude of financial institutions toward ESG related activities will probably change faster than usual. In general, financial institutions' willingness to adopt a more environmental and social friendly approach under a tight regulatory environment might be due to a couple of reasons which can be listed as.

- Avoid paying fines for not meeting the criteria set by either government or the financial / banking authority.
- To be able to access less costly funds which can be due to either.
    - o Better publicity and better sentiment scores in the public eye.
    - o Gaining access to more funds available to the institutions with better ESG scores
- If tax scheme becomes proportional to ESG of portfolio than simply to increase net profit by gaining overall tax cuts.

Following financial institutions example, customers of those institutions may also follow the same suit to be able to gain access to more economically favorable funds. Therefore, by just regulating financial system governments may regulate most of the economic activities without any additional regulations. To give some insights the case of a deposit bank can be analyzed. However, keep in mind such an analysis can be extended to the case of any financial institution. Bank in the following example can be defined as an institution that collects deposits and takes loans from other institutions (and to some extent from Central Bank) to create resources and lends these resources to the other agents to gain interest rates ultimately to make profits. Additionally offers services (money transfers, safe-keeping, payment services as intermediaries, investment accounts, intermediaries for public offerings, pension funds etc.…) for additional income. All these actions are usually free of any constraints concerning ESG criteria therefore when Banks make decision to utilize their funds there are no real incentives for them to pursue ESG criteria. How we fit sustainable finance in the Banks' problem (or in a more general sense financial institutions and firms' problem) is crucial here. In practice sustainable finance activities usually exercised through project finance or financing of certain desirable actions (e.g., using environment friendly inputs in production processes). Banks and other financial institutions are usually just there to facilitate the funding of such activities while not making environmental and social criteria as an internal part of their problem.

To push both financial institutions and companies to actively strive for ESG positive practices it is not enough to incentivize sustainability related projects, we should adopt a wholesome approach that rewards all kind of ESG positive actions and companies while punishing the ESG negative ones. Government guarantees may solve the financing problem of "some" projects while leaving other ESG or SDG goals to be unaffected or under financed. Such guarantees would also rarely affect the business-as-usual activities and are unlikely to slow down environmental and social degradation. Unlike one-by-one project finance a taxing scheme would collectively prioritize any ESG positive activity while giving the priority to the highest ranking ESG activities and companies due to their huge impact on the overall ESG score might be a better choice. Since it can crowd out financial resources supplied to ESG negative companies/ sectors simply because institutions wouldn't prefer to pay higher taxes in general as a punishment for having an ESG negative portfolio.

The most important advantage of such an incentive scheme is, it will make companies think twice about their ESG related decisions within the organization. Imagine a company that is rewarded by tax schemes for prioritizing gender equality in workplace or wage equality between different positions (upper management and blue collar). If that reward scheme is done over general performance of ESG than, company's only chance to enjoy positive incentives would not be just investing environmental related projects but to pursue overall ESG score improvement. Current regulations only reward the sustainability projects or penalizes negative externalities[11] for negligent behavior but existence of ESG friendly workstyle rarely result with positive financial gains. Under such a regime both financial institutions and other private sector companies can enjoy the positive incentives. Financial sector can be the driving force behind such a scheme. By introducing ESG score of Bank's portfolios into its problem we would not only create incentives for sustainability projects we can also create extra funds for all ESG positive practices.

One caveat of such a regulation on finance sector could be its negative discrimination against inherently low ESG industries like mining or agriculture. To prevent such negative discrimination each sector can be considered by its relative capabilities. For example, a company producing wind energy with full ESG score (let's call it ESG-100) and a company in mining sector with ESG-100 score are different, but both are the best ESG performer of their respective sector therefore they can be treated similarly from the regulatory perspective.

Other possible modifications that we can consider influencing financial institutions choice on portfolio might be through influencing capital adequacy ratios. Financial regulations may target components of capital adequacy ratios and make them sensitive to the ESG score of the portfolio of the Bank. Such modifications, if arranged thoroughly, might have similar affects to the one proposed with taxes. Incentives to required reserves and capital adequacy ratio might do the same trick as taxes. Banks can use gains from excess capital and excess reserves to supply new credits regardless of which credit the excess capacity is originated from. In any case it will continue allocate its resources between the two types of customers and activities and the final composition of its portfolio will be determined by what kind of punishment – incentive schema is chosen by government and the regulatory body.

The Case of Non – Financial Competitors

There exist other non-financial institutions that assumes some of banking activities without being considered or treated as a bank. These are insurance

11 In some countries companies of relevant size are legally obliged to hire workers from certain backgrounds but most companies prefer to pay the fines instead of hiring such individuals, if incorporated to ESG score such obligations might have a bigger impact.

and mortgage companies, investment banks, consumer credit or consumer finance companies and finally huge retailers that offer payment schemes to their customers. These institutions are not considered as banks since they do not collect deposits therefore, they are not bounded by rr or capital adequacy ratio needs but they are subject to varying degrees of financial regulation. Among them MFIs are still regulated more strictly than the consumer credit companies, and portfolios of insurance, investment or other financial companies can still be subjected to ESG related regulations mentioned at previous sections.

On the other hand, huge retailers like Amazon, Alibaba or similar companies that are strong in their respective local markets (i.e. Zalando in Germany, Vente-Privée in France or Trendyol in Turkey) are starting to receive financial income. This is because huge retailers are also starting to establish their own payment services and for these services, they neither need to be subjected to same constraints as MFIs nor need to collect deposits and carry its cost. Therefore, in general they carry lower costs for financing their customers. If such treatment is allowed in case of ESG regulation for the financial activities, then such companies will not carry any limitations for financing regular economic activities as opposed to sustainable activities.

In any case existence of such unregulated companies trying to increase their own profit and portion from the financial sector is problematic for reaching ESG goals. Unfortunately, their resources cannot be directed to desirable activities without direct intervention or additional taxation schemes. In an ideal world that wouldn't matter because it will only change the hands in which profit from financial activities accumulates. However, in an economic system where development of ESG criteria will be coordinated through financial sector such fund syphoning will ultimately leave less resources that can be directed to the ESG goals or creation of support mechanism for ESG negative firms and economic activities.

Conclusion / Further Discussion

Last three decades have witnessed huge changes in the political sociological and technological environment and we expect next three decades to be pregnant for even greater changes. The topics that have been discussed throughout this chapter and in general this book is a testament to those changes. It is our responsibility to take necessary actions by drawing lessons from the examples presented in this book and many others in the literature. Although a desire to redefine existing economic and social relationships have been voiced on many occasions by many actors concerns for not being able to meet even the most basic requirements for sustainable development goals are growing.

In this chapter the sources of change that threatens sustainable development goals and regulatory changes that can be introduced to financial sector which might make goals possible were discussed. In summary it requires ESG criteria to be placed at the hearth of decision-making process of each economic agent. Since regulating actions of every economic agent is a near impossible task this decision-making process can be introduced to lives of each agent via making it a parameter that should be accounted for while accessing the financial services. Introducing ESG criteria (or something similar) to the profit maximization problem financial institutions offers a short cut for general steering of the whole economy towards a more environmental and social equality friendly direction. The methods and regulation objectives recommended in this chapter does not just favor projects dedicated to ESG objectives they also reward the overall ESG performance of portfolio of financial institutions. This is because financial firms seek "better" customers which means they search for the customers with better incomes or firms with higher profits to lend. Unfortunately, poor debtors, low-income groups or companies that aims workplace equality over profit are not in their priority list. Therefore, regulations aiming finance sector should ensure that such a change in priority list guarantees a higher profit for the financial institution as well and this chapter tries to mention some ways to do this.

Further discussion on the implementation of the financial regulation and how it can help adopting ESG criteria may include wide range of topics. First and foremost, for such an idea to be successful we need to be able to construct an ESG performance criteria that is universal or at least universal in the main contents of the criteria. This is because it wouldn't help government to issue taxes on the ESG performance of a portfolio for each financial institution if each of them follows its own methodology. Thus, either states have to attach an ESG score for each firm and credit type by itself, or it must outsource it to the independent rating agencies that are standardized in evaluating ESG scores of companies and products. Most likely it will be a mix of the two regulatory bodies will have to draw the outline on how to calculate ESG scores and let the independent rating agencies to do it. Obviously in such a system regulatory institution will have to audit the rating agency as well. Another useful extension might be the formulation of theoretical background of the above idea. As you can see above deductions are still on the stage of idea and still waiting to be mathematically formulated. Such a theoretical formulation can also help us test the hypothesis behind the idea. Finally, the case of non-financial competitors can be discussed thoroughly and can be implemented into this theoretical problem.

Recent initiatives for responsible banking, finance or any other responsible industry trend are messengers for an upcoming change and we should expect widespread adoption of such criteria in the next few decades. An entire redesign of economic activities is on the way (or should be on the way if we want to ensure sustainability) a takeover instead of a makeover of the economic system so to speak. Best way to prepare for it is to adapt environmental, social, and governing principles into the hearth of our financial system.

Bibliography

Acar, G. (2008). Enformasy on Sistemler in Stratejik Önemi ve Planlaması. *Yönetim Bilimleri Dergisi* 6(1), 53–75.

Accenture (2020). How is COVID-19 changing the retail consumer? Data-driven insights in to consumer behavior COVID-19 Consumer Pulse Research—Wave7, Agust 2020, https://www.accenture.com/_acnmedia/PDF-130/Accenture-Retail-Research-POV-Wave-Seven.pdf#zoom=40, 16/10/2021.

Acemoglu, D., & Pascual, R. (2019). Automation and new tasks: How technology displaces and reinstates llabor. *Journal of Economic Perspectives* 33(2), 3–30.

Ak, Ş., Gökdaş, İ., Öksüz, C., & Torun, F. (2021). Uzaktan eğitimde eğiticilerin eğitimi: Uzaktan eğitime yönelik öz yeterlik ve yarar algısına etkisi. *Açıköğretim Uygulamaları ve Araştırmaları Dergisi* (AUAd) 7(1), 24–44.

Akbaş, Ö. Z., & Dursun, C. (2020). Koronavirüs (Covid-19) pandemisi sürecinde Özel alanına kamusal alanı sığdıran çalışan anneler. *Avrasya Sosyal ve Ekonomi Araştırmaları Dergisi (ASEAD)/Eurasian Journal of Researches in Social and Economics (EJRSE),* 7(5), 78–94 ISSN:2148-9963. Retrieved From: https://dergipark.org.tr/tr/download/article-file/1128136

Akçi, Y., & ve Annaç Göv, S. (2015). Tüketicilerin e-ticaret algılarının incelenmesi (Gaziantep ve Adıyaman örneği). Mehmet Akif Ersoy Üniversitesi Sosyal Bilimler Enstitüsü Dergisi, 7(13), 413–433.

Alkoy, S. (2003). Olası biyolojik silah olarak yeniden gündeme gelen eski hastalık: Çiçek. *TTB Sürekli Tıp Eğitimi Dergisi*, 12(7), 246, 247.

Akhtar, N., Akhtar, M. N., Usman, M., Ali, M. S., & Umar I. (2020). COVID-19 restrictions and consumers' psychological reactance toward offline shopping freedom restoration. *The Service Industries Journal*, 40(13–14), 891–913.

Akın, F. (2020). Dijital dönüşümün bankacılık sektörü üzerindeki etkileri. *Balkan ve Yakın Doğu Sosyal Bilimler Dergisi*, 6(2), 15–27.

Alon, T., Doepke, M., Olmstead-Rumsey, J., & Tertilt, M. (2020). *The impact of Covid-19 on gender equality.* [Online] Available at: http://www.nber.org/papers/w26947 [Accessed 02 08 2021].

Altıparmak, M. (2011). E-öğrenme ve uzaktan eğitimde açık kaynak kodlu öğrenme yönetim sistemleri. Malatya: Akademik Bilişim'11–XIII. Akademik Bilişim Konferansı Bildirileri Kitabı, 319–327.

Alvaredo, F., Atkinson, A. B., Piketty, T., & Saez, E. (2013). The top 1 percent in international and historical perspective. *Journal of Economic Perspectives* 27, 3–20.

Andrew, A., Cattan, S., Costa Dias, M., Farquharson,C., Kraftman, L., Krutikova, S., Phimister, A., & ve Sevilla, A. (2020). "How Are Mothers and Fathers Balancing Work and Family Under Lockdown?". Institute for Fiscal Studies. https://www.ifs.org.uk/uploads/BN290-Mothers-andfathers-balancing-work-and-life-under-lockdown.pdf. Erişim Tarihi: 11.01.2021

Angelopoulos, K., Economides, G., & Kammas, P. (2007). Tax-spending policies and economic growth: theoretical predictions and evidence from the OECD. *European Journal of Political Economy,* 23(4), 885–902. Web.

Antalyalı, Ö. L. (2004). Distance Education Perception and Operations Research Course Distance Education Isparta: Süleyman Demirel University Institute of Social Sciences Unpublished Master's Thesis.

Aral, N., & Doğan-Keskin, A. (2018). Ebeveyn bakış açısıyla 0-6 yaş dönemimde teknolojik alet kullanımının incelenmesi. *Addicta;Turksh Jaurnal on Addiction*, 5(2), 317–348. Retrieved From: https://app.trdizin.gov.tr/publication/paper/detail/TXpFeE9EYzBOQT09

Arar, A. (1999). "Historical Development of Distance Education, Distance Education Application Models and Costs", The First Distance Education Symposium was held on November 15–16, 1999. Ankara: Land Forces Training and Doctrine Command.

Armstrong, M., & Taylor, S. (2014). *Armstrong's Handbook of Human Resource Management Practice.* Kogan Page.

Arner, D. W., Barberis, J. N., Walker, J., Buckley, R. P., Dahdal, A. M., & Zetzsche, D. A. (2020). Digital finance & the COVID-19 crisis. *University of Hong Kong Faculty of Law Research Paper*, (2020/017).

Arthur, J. W., Bennett, J. W., Edens, P. S., & Bell, S. T. (2003). Effectiveness of training in organizations: A meta-analysis of design and evaluation features. *Journal of Applied Pscyhology,* 88(2), 234–245.

Artuc, E., Paulo, B., & Rijkers, B. (2018). "Robots, Tasks and Trade." In *Policy Research Working Paper Series 8674.* Washington DC, US: The World Bank.

Atkinson, A. B., Thomas, P., & Emmanuel, S. (2011). Top incomes in the long run of history. *Journal of Economic Literature,* 49, 3–71.

Austin, P. L. (2020). What'Preppers' can teach us about dealing with the corona virus Outbreak, Time, https://time.com/5797950/coronavirus-preppers/.

Autor, D. H., Katz, L. F., & Krueger, A. B. (1998). Computing inequality: Have computers changed the labor market? *The Quarterly Journal of Economics,* 113(4), 1169–1213.

Aygün, Ş. S., Atalay, N., Kılıç, Z., & Yaşar, S. (2016). Öğretmen adaylarına yönelik 21. yüzyıl becerileri yeterlilik algıları ölçeğinin geliştirilmesi: geçerlik ve güvenirlik çalışması. *Pamukkale Üniversitesi Eğitim Fakültesi Dergisi,* 40(40),

160–175. Retrieved From https://dergipark.org.tr/tr/pub/pauefd/issue/33883/375190

Aykar, A. N., & Yurdakal, İ. H. (2021). Erken çocukluk öğretmenlerinin acil uzaktan eğitime ilişkin görüşleri. *Temel Eğitim Dergisi*, 3(2), 6–14. Retrieved From: https://doi.org/10.52105/temelegitim.3.2.1

Bankalararası Kart Merkezi, Kartlı Harcama Verileri. https://bkm.com.tr/raporlar-ve-yayinlar/donemsel-bilgiler/

Barney, J. (1991). Firm resources and sustained competitive advantage. *Journal of Management,* 17(1), 99–120.

Bartodziej C. J. (2015). *The Concept Industry 4.0: An Empirical Analysis of Technologies and Applications in Production Logistics.* Wiesbaden: Springer Gabler.

Barua, B., & Barua, S. (2021). COVID-19 implications for banks: evidence from an emerging economy. *SN Business & Economics*, *1*(1), 1–28.

Bayar, A. A., Günçavdı, Ö., & ve Levent, H. (2020). *Politika raporu: COVID-19 salgınının kadınların çalışma ve hane yaşamı üzerine etkileri.* İstanbul: İstanbul Politik Araştırmalar Enstitüsü.

Billing, Y. D. (2011). Are women in management victims of the phantom of the male norm?. *Gender, Work and Organization,* *18*(3), May, 298–317.

Bissola, R., & Imperatori, B. (2018). HRM 4.0: The digital transformation of the HR department. In F. Cantoni, & G. Mangia (Eds.), *Human Resource Management and Digitalization*. London: Routledge.

Boffo, R., & Patalano, R. (2020). *ESG Investing: Practices, Progress and Challenges.* OECD Paris. https://www.oecd.org/finance/ESG-Investing-Practices-Progress-Challenges.pdf

Bogliacino, F., Piva, M., & Vivarelli, M. (2011). R&D and employment: Some evidence from European microdata. *IZA Discussion Papers*, 5908. Bonn, Germany: IZA.

Bonekamp, L., & Sure, M. (2015). Consequences of industry 4.0 on human labour and work organization. *Journal of Business and Media Psychology*, 6(1), 33–40.

Bonnet, F., Carré, F., Chen, M., & Vanek, J. (2021). *Home-based Workers in the World: A Statistical Profile.* s.l.: Women in Informal Employment: Globalizing and Organizing.

Boughton, J. M. (2001). Was Suez in 1956 the first financial crisis of the twenty-first century? *Finance & Development, September 2001, 38*(3)

Bouma, J. J., Marcel, J., & Leon, K. (Eds.) (2017). *Sustainable Banking. The Greening of Finance.* New York, US: Routledge (First published: 2001 by Sheffield: Greenleaf Publishing).

Bozkurt, A. (2020). Koronavirüs (Covid-19) pandemi süreci ve pandemi sonrası dünyada eğitime yönelik değerlendirmeler: Yeni normal ve yeni eğitim paradigması. *Açıköğretim Uygulamaları ve Araştırmaları Dergisi,* 6(3), 112–142. Retrieved From https://dergipark.org.tr/en/pub/auad/issue/56247/773769

Bozkurt, A., Jung, I., Xiao, J., Vladimirschi, V., Schuwer, R., Egorov, G., & Paskevicius, M. (2020). A global outlook to the interruption of education due to COVID-19 Pandemic: Navigating in a time of uncertainty and crisis. *Asian Journal of Distance Education,* 15(1), 1–126. Retrieved From: http://www.asianjde.com/ojs/index.php/AsianJDE/article/view/462/307

Brannon, L. (2011). *Gender: Psychological Perspectives. 6e.*. Boston: Pearson.

Bretz, R. D., & Judge, T. A. (1998). Realistic job previews: A test of the adverse self-selection hypothesis. *Journal of Applied Psychology,* 83(2), 330–337.

Brom, C., Lukavský, J., Greger, D., Hannemann, T., Straková, J., & Švarícek, R. (2020). Mandatory home education during the COVID-19 lockdown in the Czech Republic: A rapid survey of 1st-9th graders' parents. *Frontiers in Education,* 5(103), 1–8. Retrieved From: https://www.frontiersin.org/articles/10.3389/feduc.2020.00103/full

Bryant, C. H., Saurabh S., & Dilip W. (2020). *How Artificial Intelligence Will Impact K-12.* McKinsey&Company.

Brynjolfsion, E., & McAfee, A. (2011). *The Second Machine Age, Work, Progress and Prosperity in a Time of Brilliant Technologies.* New York: Norton & Company Press.

Buchanan, J. M., & William, S. C. (1962). Externality. *Economica,* 29, 371–384.

Buluk, B., & Eşitti, B. (2020). Koronavirüs (Covid-19) sürecinde uzaktan eğitimin turizm lisans öğrencileri tarafından değerlendirilmesi. *Journal of Awareness,* 5(3), 285–298. doı: 10.26809/joa.5.021. Retrieved From: https://journals.gen.tr/joa. DOİ: https://doi.org/10.26809/joa.5.021

Burma, Z. A. (2014). Human resource management and its importance for today's organizations. *International Journal of Education and Social Science,* 1(2), 85–94.

Cabı, E. (2018). Teaching computer literacy via distance education: Experiences of the instructors. *Başkent University Journal of Education,* 5(1), 61–68.

Calp, M. H., & Doğan, A. (2019). İnsan kaynakları yönetiminde dijital dönüşüm. Uluslararası Bilimler Akademisi, Sosyal Bilimler Tam Metin Kitabı, 387–400.

Can, E. (2020). Coronavirüs (Covid-19) pandemisi ve pedagojik yansımaları: Türkiye'de açık ve uzaktan eğitim uygulamaları. *Açıköğretim Uygulamaları ve Araştırmaları Dergisi,* 6(2), 11–53. Retrieved From https://dergipark.org.tr/tr/pub/auad/issue/55662/761354

Capgemini. (2020). The consumer of Covid-19: Global consumer sentiment research in the consumer products and retail industry, Research Note, April, 1–15.

Carletti, E., Claessens, S., Fatás, A., & Vives, X. (2020). *Post-Covid-19 World.* Centre for Economic Policy Research. UK ISBN: 978-1-912179-34-3. https://media.iese.edu/research/pdfs/ST-0549-E.pdf

Caruso, L. (2018). Digital innovation and the fourth industrial revolution-epochal social changes. *AI & Soc,* 33(3), 379–392.

Caterall, M., & Maclaran, P. (2002). Gender perspectives in consumer behaviour: An overview and future directions. *The Marketing Review, 2,* 405–425.

Chang, H. Y. (2009). Employee turnover: A novel prediction solution with effective feature selection. *WSEAS Transactions on Information Science and Applications,* 6(3), 252–256.

Charles Schwab Corparaiton. (2019). Annual Report, https://content.schwab.com/web/retail/public/about-schwab/schwab_annual_report_2019.pdf

Chmielewska, B. et al. (2021). Effects of the COVID-19 pandemic on maternal and perinatal outcomes: A systematic review and meta-analysis. *Lancet Global Health,* 9(6), 759–772.

Coase, R. H. (1960). The problem of social cost. *Journal of Law and Economics,* 3, 1–44.

Coleman, J. S. (1988). Social capital in the creation of human capital. *American Journal of Sociology,* 94, 95–120.

COP 21. (2015). *The Paris Agreement.* Accessible at: https://unfccc.int/sites/default/files/ english_paris_ agreement.pdf

Credit Union Magazine. (2020). Ecommerce in the world of Covid-19, Summer. https://pubs.royle.com/publication/?m=62956&i=661725&p=4&ver=html5

Currie, J., & Almond, D. (2011). *Human Capital Development before Age Five.* Handbook of labor economics (Vol. 4, pp. 1315–1486). Amsterdam: Elsevier.

Çakıroğlu, Ü., & Taşkın, N. (2016). Teaching numbers to preschool students with ınteractive multimedia: An experimental study. *Cukurova University Faculty of Education Journal,* 45(1), 1–22. Retrieved from https://dergipark.org.tr/en/pub/cuefd/issue/27005/283882

Çaykuş, E. T., & Mutlu-Çaykuş, T. (2020). Covid-19 pandemi sürecinde çocukların psikolojik dayanıklılığını güçlendirme yolları: ailelere, öğretmenlere ve ruh sağlığı uzmanlarına öneriler. *Avrasya Sosyal ve Ekonomi Araştırmaları Dergisi, COVID-19 Özel Sayısı,* 2, 95–113. Retrieved From: https://dergipark.org.tr/tr/pub/asead/issue/54658/738573

Çoban, S. (2013). *The Development of Distance and Technology-Supported Education*. Istanbul: XVI. Proceedings of the Internet Conference in Turkey.

Çukadar, S., & ve Çelik, S. (2003). Distance education and university libraries based on the internet. Journal of Doğuş University, 4(1), 33.

Da Silva, I. M., Lordello, S. R., Schmidt, B., & De Melo Mietto, G. S.(2020). Brazilian families facing the covid-19 outbreak. *Journal of Comparative Family Studies*, 51(3–4), 324–336. doi:10.3138/jcfs.3-4.008

Dahl, R. (2010). Greenwashing: Do you know what you're buying? *Environmental Health Perspectives*, 118 (6), 246–252.

Dang, H.-A. H., & Nguyen, C. V. (2021). Genderinequalityduringthe COVID-19 pandemic: Income, expenditure, savings, and jobloss. *World Development*, 140, 1–10. https://doi.org/10.1016/j.worlddev.2020.105296.

Das, S., Barik, R., & Mukherje, A. (2020). Salary prediction using regression techniques. *Engineering Research Network (EngRN)*, 35(2), 1–5.

Day, Ü. & Çilingir, C. (2021). *Çalışma hayatında cinsiyet ve ücret eşitliği*. [Online] Available at: https://www.pwc.com.tr/calisma-hayatinda-cinsiyet-ucret-esitligi [Accessed 14 07 2021].

Deloitte. (2020). Küresel Covid-19 Salgınının Türkiye'de Farklı Kategorilere Etkileri- II, Deloitte Yayınları.

Demirgüç-Kunt, A., Pedraza, A., & Ruiz-Ortega, C. (2021). Banking sector performance during the COVID-19 crisis. *Journal of Banking & Finance*, 133, 106305.

Devrim, F. (2001). Küreselleşen Krizler ve Türkiye. *Yeni Türkiye Dergisi, Ekonomik Kriz Özel Sayısı*, 2, 939–945.

Di Giorgio, E. Di Riso, D., Mioni, G., & Cellini N. (2020). The interplay between mothers' and children behavioral and psychological factors during Covid 19: An Italian study Preprint. doi: org/10.31234/osf.io/dqk7h

Dietrich, G., & Livingston, G. (2012). *Marketing in the Round, the Digital Era*. USA: Que Publishing.

DİSK-AR (2021a). *DİSK-AR salgının bilançosunu çıkardı: 3,6 milyon istihdam kaybı!*. [Online] Available at: http://disk.org.tr/2021/08/disk-ar-salginin-bilancosunu-cikardi-36-milyon-istihdam-kaybi/ [Accessed 01 09 2021].

DİSK-AR (2021b). *Yasak kalktı, ekonomi açıldı, işsizlik fırladı!*. [Online] Available at: http://arastirma.disk.org.tr/?p=7794 [Accessed 01 09 2021].

Doğan, A. (2011). Elektronik insan kaynakları yönetimi ve fonksiyonları. Internet Uygulamaları ve Yönetim Dergisi, 2(2), 52–80. doi: https://doi.org/10.1108/IJOEM-12-2020-1530, pp. 1–20.

Dong, C. Cao, S., & Li, H. (2020). Young children's online learning during COVID-19 pandemic: Chinese parents' beliefs and attitudes. *Children and Youth Services Review*, 118105440. Retrieved From: https://doi.org/10.1016/j.childyouth.2020.105440

DORinsight. (2020, Nisan 29). Türkiye'deki koronavirüs salgını sürecinde yapılan ankete katılanların %63'ü yaz tatili yapmayı planlamıyor. Aralık 4, 2020 Dorinsight Haberleri: https://www.haberler.com/dorinsight.

Durmaz, Y., Bahar Reyhan, O., & ve Kurtlar, M. (2020, Haziran 1). Kişisel faktörlerin tüketici satın alma davranışlarına etkisi üzerine bir araştırma. Akademik Yaklaşımlar Dergisi, 114–133.

Döğer, S. S. & Kılınç, F. E. (2021). Okul öncesi dönemdeki çocukların kovid-19 pandemisinde ev karantinası yaşamları. *Türkiye Sağlık Araştırmaları Dergisi*, 2(2), 1–14. Retrieved From https://dergipark.org.tr/tr/pub/tjhr/issue/62983/875799

Drath, R., & Horch, A. (2014). Industrie 4.0: Hit or hype? *IEEE Industrial Electronics Magazine*, *8*, 56–58. https://doi.org/10.1109/MIE.2014.2312079.

Drucker P. F. (1999). Knowledge-worker productivity: The biggest challenge. *California Review Management, 41*(2), 79–94.

Duman, A. (2020). Wage Losses and Inequality in Developing Countries: Labor market and distributional consequences of Covid-19 lockdowns in Turkey. *GLO Discussion,* Issue 602.

Eagly, A., & Carli, L. (2007). *Through the Labrinth: The Truth about How Women become Leaders.* Boston: Harvard Business Press.

Eger, L., Komarkova, L., Egerova, D., & Michal, M. (2021). Theeffect of COVID-19 on consumershoppingbehaviour: Generationalcohortperspective. Journal of Retailingand Consumer Services, 61, 1–11. https://doi.org/10.1016/j.jretconser.2021.102542.

Elkington, J. (1998). Accounting for the triple bottom line. *Measuring Business Excellence* 2, 18–22.

Ellison, B., McFadden, B., Rickard, B. J., & Wilson, N. L. W. (2021). Examining food purchase behavior and food values during the COVID-19 pandemic. *Applied Economic Perspectives and Policy*, 43(1), 58–72.

Engel, J., Blackwell, R., & Miniard, P. (1995). *Consumer Behaviour. 8e..* Orlando, FL: The Dryden Press.

Erkan, İ. (2020). Consumers' perceptions of unity solidarity and motivation themed advertisements published in the Covid-19 period. *Gaziantep University Journal of Social Sciences 2020 Special Issue*, 585– 600. doi:https://doi.org/10.21547/jss.788085

Erkan, S., & Kırca, A. (2010). Okul öncesi eğitimin ilköğretim birinci sınıf öğrencilerinin okula hazır bulunuşluklarına etkisinin incelenmesi. *Hacettepe Üniversitesi Eğitim Fakültesi Dergisi*, 38(38), 94–106. Retrieved from https://dergipark.org.tr/tr/pub/hunefd/issue/7798/102150

Eubanks, B. (2019). *Artificial Intelligence for HR Use AI to Support and Develop a Successful Workforce*. U.S.A.: Kogan Press.

European Commission, n.d. *Statistics: What the Commission is doing*. [Online] Available at: https://ec.europa.eu/info/topics/statistics_en [Accessed 06 03 2021].

European Commission. (2018). *EU Action Plan: Financing Sustainable Growth*. Brussels: European Commission. https://eur-lex.europa.eu/legal-content/EN/TXT/?uri=CELEX:52018DC0097

European Union. (2021). Digital Education Action Plan (2021–2027). https://education.ec.europa.eu/focus-topics/digital-education/action-plan

Eurostat. (2021). *Employment rates by sex, age and citizenship (%)*. [Online] Available at: https://ec.europa.eu/eurostat/databrowser/view/lfsa_ergan/default/table?lang=en [Accessed 25 05 2021].

Eurostat. (2021). Gender pay gap statistics. [Online] Available at: https://ec.europa.eu/eurostat/statistics-explained/index.php?title=Gender_pay_gap_statistics#:~:text=gender%20pay%20gap-,Gender% 20pay%20gap%20levels%20vary%20significantly%20across%20EU,area%20(EA%2D19). [Accessed 25 06 2021].

Eyel, C. Ş. (2020). Covid-19 and remote working. In D. Hıdıroğlu, S. S. Aktuğ, & O. Yılmaz (Eds.), *Covid-19 and New Business Ecosystem*, 185–204. Ankara: Gazi Kitabevi.

Eyel, C. Ş. (2021). Uzaktan çalışma ölçeği Türkçe uyarlaması: Güvenilirlik ve geçerlilik analizi. In E. Özdoğlar, & R. Aliyev (Eds.), *1. Uluslararası Arslantepe bilimsel araştırmalar kongresi kongre kitabı*, 231–244. Ankara: İKSAD.

Ferri, F., Grifoni, P., & Guzzo, T. (2020). Online learning and emergency remote teaching: Opportunities and challenges in emergency situations. *Societies*, 10(86), 1–18. doi:10.3390/soc10040086. Retrieved From: www.mdpi.com/journal/societies

Fettig, K., Gaedi, T., Köskal, A., Kühn, A., & Stuber, F. (2018). *Impact of industry 4.0 on organizational structures*. 2018 IEEE International Conference on Engineering, 1–8.

Ford, M. (2018). *Robotların yükselişi*. İstanbul: Kronik Yayıncılık.

Ford, M. (2015). *The Rise of the Robots: Technology and the Threat of a Jobless Future*. New York, US: Basic Books.

Frey, C. B., & Michael, O. (2013). *The Future of Employment. How Susceptible are Jobs to Computerization*. Mimeo: Oxford Martin School.

Friede, G., Busch, T., & Bassen, A. (2015). ESG and financial performance: Aggregated evidence from more than 2000 empirical studies. *Journal of Sustainable Finance and Investment* 5(4), 210–233.

Friedman, M. (2002). *Capitalism and Freedom*. Chicago ve Londra: Fourtieth Anniversary Edition. Chicago Üniversitesi Yayınları.

Garg, S., Sinha, S., Kar, A. K., & Mani, M. (2021). A review of machine learning applications in human resource management. *International Journal of Productivity and Performance Management*.

Gemmell, N., Richard, K., & Ismael, S. (2014). The growth effects of tax rates in the OECD. *Canadian Journal of Economics/Revue canadienne d'èconomique*, 47, 1217–1255.

George, M. G., Elizabeth, C., Johanna, C., Peter, C., & Martin, W. (2016). *Technology at Work v2. 0: The Future is not What It Used to Be*. Oxford, UK: CityGroup and University of Oxford.

Georgescu-Roegen, N. (1975). Energy and economic myths. *Southern Economic Journal. Tennessee: Southern Economic Association*, 41(3), 347–81.

Gera, P. (2017). Banking as a living business, Accenture, https://www.accenture.com/_acnmedia/pdf-65/accenture-banking-as-a-livingbusiness-2017.pdf [Erişim Tarihi: 13.11.2020].

Giannini, S., & Lewis, G. S. (2020). Three ways to plan for equity during the coronavirus school closures. Retrieved From: https://gemreportunesco.wordpress.com/2020/03/25/three-ways-to-plan-forequity-during-the-coronavirus-school-closures/

Giddens, A. (2018). Kapitalizm ve Modern Sosyal Teori (7. Baskı), (Çev. Ümit Tatlıcan), İletişim Yayınları, İstanbul.

Goswami, S., & Vineet, C. (2021). Impact of change in consumerbehaviourandneedprioritisationon retailindustry in Rajasthanduring COVID-19 pandemic. *MaterialsToday: Proceedings*, 46(20), 10262–10267.

Görçün, Ö. F. (2017). *Dördüncü endüstri devrimi "Endüstri 4.0"*. İstanbul: Beta Basım A.Ş.

Grand View Research, Inc. Technology (2020). *Education Technology Market Size, Share & Trends Analysis Report*. https://www.grandviewresearch.com/info/reports-and-publications

Greengard, S. (1994). Data-base and software integration: Allowing HR to work more efficiently. *Personnel Journal*, 45–46.

Greenhalg, C., Mark, L., & Bosworth, D. (2001). Technological activity and employment in a panel of UK firms. *Scottish Journal of Political Economy*, 48, 260–82.

Gupta, R., Nair, K., & Radhakrishnan, L. (2021). Impact of COVID-19 crisis on stocking and impulse buying behaviour of consumers. *International Journal of Social Economics*, 48(12), 1794–1809.

Guthrie, C., Fosso-Wamba, S., & Arnaud, J. B. (2021). Online consumer resilience during a pandemic: An exploratory study of e-commerce behavior before, during and after a COVID-19 lockdown. *Journal of Retailing and Consumer Services*, 61.

Günay, D., Öcal, A., & ve Öcalan, K. (2018). Sanayi ve sanayi tarihi. Mimar ve Mühendis Dergisi, 31, 8–14 akt. Dördüncü sanayi devriminin emek piyasaları üzerindeki olası etkilerinin incelenmesi ve çözüm önerileri. Uluslararası Toplum Araştırması Dergisi, 2071.

Güven, H. (2020). Covid-19 sürecinde e-ticaret sitelerine yöneltilen müşteri şikâyetlerinin incelenmesi. *Turkish Studies*, 15(4), 511–530. doi:http://dx.doi.org/10.7827/TurkishStudies.44354

Habsbawn, E. J. (2013). *Sanayi ve imparatorluk*. Ankara: Dost Yayınevi.

Haijian, L., & Fangfang, Z. (2018). Employee transition and future outlook evolution from employee 1 to employee 4. *China Economist*, 13(3), 78–87.

Handy, C. (1984). *The Future of Work-a Guide to a Changing Society*. Oxford: Oxford Press.

Hardin, G. (1968). The tragedy of the commons. *Science*, 162 (3859), 1243–1248.

Harley, D. (2002). Planning for an uncertain future: A US perspective on why accurate predictions about ICTs may be difficult. *Journal of Studies in International Education*, 6(2), 172–187.

Hartwick, J. M. (1990). Natural resources, national accounting and economic depreciation. *Journal of Public Economics*, 43(3), 291–304.

Hecklau, F., Galeitzke, M., Flachs, S., & Kohl H. (2016). Holistic approach for human resource management in industry 4.0. *Procedia CIRP*, 54(1), 1–6.

Heckman, J., Pinto, R., & Savelyev, P. (2013). Understanding the mechanisms through which an influential early childhood program boosted adult outcomes. *American Economic Review*, 103(6), 2052–86. Retrieved From: https://www.aeaweb.org/articles/pdf/doi/10.1257/aer.103.6.2052

Heo, M. (2009). Digital storytelling: An empirical study of the impact of digital storytelling on pre-service teachers' self-efficacy and dispositions towards educational technology. *Educational Multimedia and Hypermedia*, 18(4), 405–428. Retrieved From: https://www.learntechlib.org/primary/p/30458/

Higher Education Information Management System. (2020). https://istatistik.yok.gov.tr/

Hirschi, A. (2015). *Konzepte zur förderung von laufbahnentwicklung im 21. Jahrhundert*. Universität Bern.

Hochschild, A. R., & Machung, A. (2003). *The Second Shift*, 2nd ed. New York: Penguin Books.

Hodges, C., Moore, S., Lockee, B., Trust, T., & Bond, A. (2020). The difference between emergency remote teaching and online learning. *Educause Review*, 27, 1–12. Retrieved From: https://er.educause.edu/articles/2020/3/the-differencebetween-emergency-remoteteaching-and-online-learning

Hofstede, G. (2001). *Cultures Consequences: Comparing Values, Behaviours, Institutions and Organizations across Nations.* London: Sage Publications.

Hom, P. W., Griffeth, R. W., Palich, L. E., & Bracker, J. S. (1999). Revisiting met expectations as a reason why realistic job previews work. *Personnel Psychology*, *52*(2), 97–112.

Hope, D., & John, L. (2020). The economic consequences of major tax cuts for the rich. *International Inequalities Institute Working Papers* (55). London School of Economics and Political Science, London, UK.

How artificial intelligence will impact K-12 teachers . https://www.mckinsey.com/industries/public-and-social-sector/our-insights/how-artificial-intelligence-will-impact-k-12-teachers#

https://ec.europa.eu/education/education-in-the-eu/digital-education-action-plan_en#:~:text=The%20Digital%20Education%20Action%20Plan,cooperation%20at%20European%20level%20to%3A&text=make%20education%20and%20training%20systems%20fit%20for%20the%20digital%20age.

https://www.mckinsey.com/tr/our-insights/stakeholder-capitalism-report.

https://www.project-syndicate.org/commentary/small-governments-big-failure-covid19-by-mariana-mazzucato-and-giulio-quaggiotto-2020-05.

https://www.weforum.org/agenda/2020/06/now-is-the-time-for-a-great-reset/

Huang, E. Y., Lin, S. W., & Huang, T. K. (2012). What type of learning style leads to online participation in the mixed mode e-learning environment? A study of software usage instruction. *Computers & Education*, 58(1), 338–349.

Huffstetter, M., King, J. R., Onwuegbuzie, A. J., Schneider, J. J., & Powellsmith, K. A. (2010). Effects of a computer-based early reading program on the early reading and oral language skills of at-risk preschool children. *Journal of Education for Students Placed at Risk (JESPAR)*, 15(4), 279–298. doi: 10.1080/10824669.2010.532415

ICTC. (2020). *A Digital Future for Northeastern Ontario*. https://www.ictc-ctic.ca/digital-future-northeastern-ontario/

ILO. (2018). More than 60 per cent of the world's employed population are in the informal economy. [Online] Available at: https://www.ilo.org/global/about-the-ilo/newsroom/news/WCMS_627189/lang--en/index.htm#:~:text=employed%20population%20...-,More%20than%2060%20per%20cent%20of%20the%20world's%20employed%20population,work%20and%20decent%20working%20conditions. [Accessed 29 07 2021].

ILO. (2020). Cinsiyee Dayalı Ücret Farkının Ölçümü: Türkiye Uygulaması. [Online] Available at: https://www.ilo.org/wcmsp5/groups/public/---europe/---ro-geneva/---ilo-ankara/documents/publication/wcms_756659.pdf [Accessed 15 06 2021].

IMF. (2020). World Economic Outlook, Ekim 2020. https://www.imf.org/en/Publications/WEO/Issues/2020/09/30/world-economic-outlook-october-2020

IMF. (2021). World Economic Outlook, Ekim 2021. https://www.imf.org/en/Publications/WEO/weo-database/2021/October

International Labour Organization. (2013). *Women and Men in the Informal Economy: A Statistical Picture*. Geneva: International Labour Office.

Islam, T., Pitafi, A. H., Arya, V., Wang, Y., Akhtar, N., Mubarik, S., & Xiaobei, L. (2021). Panicbuying in the COVID-19 pandemic: A multi-countryexamination. *Journal of Retailingand Consumer Services*, 59, 1–13. https://doi.org/10.1016/j.jretconser.2020.102357

Iwai, Y. (2020). Online Learning during the COVID-19 Pandemic: What do we gain and what do we lose when classrooms go virtual? *Scientific American*. Retrieved From: https://blogs.scientificamerican.com/observations/online-learning-during-the-COVID-19-pandemic

İnci, M. A., & Kandır, A. (2017). Okul öncesi eğitimde dijital teknolojinin kullanımıyla ilgili bilimsel çalışmaların değerlendirilmesi, *Hitit Üniversitesi Sosyal Bilimler Enstitüsü Dergisi*, 10(2), 1705–1724. doı: 10.17218/hititsosbil.335370. Retrieved From: https://dergipark.org.tr/tr/pub/hititsosbil/issue/31476/335370

Jain, S. (2017). *Is Artificial Intelligence –the Next Big Thing in HR?* International Conference on Innovative Research in Science Technology and Management Modi Institute of Management & Technolohy, Dadabari, Kota, Rajasthan 22–23 January.

Jain, S. (2018). Human resource management and artificial intelligence. *International Journal of Management and Social Sciences Research (IJMSSR)*, *7*(3), 56–59.

Jeucken, M. (2001). *Sustainable Finance and Banking: The Financial Sector and the Future of the Planet*. UK: Earthscan Publications Ltd.

Jones, K. (2020). How technology is shaping the future of education. Retrieved From: https://www.visualcapitalist.com/how-technology-is-shaping-the-futureof-education/.

Journal of Consumer Behaviour, 3(2), 129–141.

Karacan Özdemir, N., & Ayaz, A. (2020). Endüstri 4.0 çerçevesinde kariyer gelişimini destekleme hizmetlerinin yapılandırılması: İhtiyaçlar, öncelikler ve gereklilikler. Yüksekögretim ve Bilim Dergisi, 10(1), 96–102. https://doi.org/10.5961/ihes.202Q.371

Keane, M., & Neal, T. (2021). Consumerpanic in the COVID-19 pandemic. *Journal of Econometrics*, 220, 86–105.

Kırık, A. M. (2014). Marmara Communication Journal / Marmara. University Journal of Communication • Issue / Issue: 21.

Kim, J. (2020). Learning and teaching online during COVID 19: Experiences of student teachers in an early childhood education practicum. *International Journal of Early Childhood*, 52, 145–158. doi:10.1007/s13158-020-00272-6. Retrived From: https://link.springer.com/article/10.1007/s13 158-020-00272-6

Kim, R. Y. (2020). The impact of COVID-19 on consumers: Preparing for digital sales. *IEEE Engineering Management Review*. doi: 10.1109/EMR.2020.2990115, 1–16.

King, D. L., Delfabbro, P. H., Billieux, J., & Potenza, M. N. (2020). Problematic online gaming and the Covid-19 pandemic. *Journal of Behavioral Addictions*, doi:10.1556/2006.2020.00016. Retrieved From: https://akjournals.com/view/journals/2006/9/2/article-p184.xml?body=pdf-23898

Kirk, C. P., & Rifkin, L. S. (2020). I'lltradeyoudiamondsfortoiletpaper: Consumer reacting, copingandadaptingbehaviors in the COVID-19 pandemic. *Journal of Business Research*, 117, 124–131.

Kiryakova, G. (2009). Review of distance education. *Trakia Journal of Sciences*, 7(3), 29–34. ISSN 1313–3551. Retrieved From: http://www.uni-sz.bg/

Kocaman Karoğlu, A. (2016). Okul öncesi eğitimde dijital hikâye anlatımı üzerine öğretmen görüşleri. *Turkish Online Journal of Qualitative Inquiry* (TOJQI), 7(1), 175–205. Retrieved From: https://dergipark.org.tr/en/pub/tojqi/issue/21410/229445

Kocaman, K. A. (2015). Öğretim sürecinde hikâye anlatmanin teknolojiyle değişen doğası: Dijital hikâye anlatımı. *Eğitim Teknolojisi Kuram ve Uygulama*, 5(2), 89- 106. Retrieved From: https://dergipark.org.tr/en/pub/etku/arti cle/84268

Konca, A. S., & Çakır, T. (2021). Pandemi sürecinde uzaktan eğitim ile okul öncesi eğitimden ilkokula geçiş hakkında veli görüşleri. *Yaşadıkça Eğitim*, 35(2), 520–545. Retrieved From: http://journals.iku.edu.tr/yed/index.php/yed/article/view/307

KPMG. (2017). *The changing landscape of disruptive technologies*, Part 2, Innovation Convergence Unlocks New Paradigms Report.

Kundu, B., & Bhowmik, D. (2020). Societal impact of novel corona virus (COVID 19 pandemic) in India. doi: 10.31235/osf.io/vm5rz. Retrieved From https://osf.io/preprints/socarxiv/vm5rz/

Kurt Demirbaş, N., & Sevgili Koçak, S. (2020). 2-6 yaş arasında çocuğu olan ebeveynlerin bakış açısıyla Covid 19 salgın sürecinin değerlendirilmesi. *Avrasya Sosyal ve Ekonomi Araştırmaları Dergisi*, 7(6), 328–349. Retrieved From: https://dergipark.org.tr/en/pub/asead/issue/55211/750920

Kuznets, S. (1955). Economic growth and income inequality. *American Economic Review*, 45 (March), 1–28.

Landes, S. (1998). Kapitalizmin Doğuşu, (çev. Süleyman E. Gündüz). İstanbul: İnsan Yayınları, 2. baskı.

Lane, M., & Anne, S.- M. (2021). The impact of artificial intelligence on the labour market: What do we know so far? *OECD Social, Employment and Migration Working Papers*, No. 256, Paris, France.

Lavidas, K., Katsidima, M., Theodoratou, S., Komis, V., & Nikolopoulou, K. (2021). Preschool teachers' perceptions about TPACK in Greek educational context. *Journal Of Computers In Education*. Retrieved From: https://doi.org/10.1007/s40692-021-00184-x

Lavuri, R. (2021). Intrinsic factors affecting online impulsive shopping during the COVID-19 in emerging markets. *International Journal of Emerging Markets*, ahead-of-print.

Lawrence, P. (2020). Global capitalism and Africa after Covid-19. *Review of African Political Economy*, 47(165), 351–362. doi: 10.1080/03056244.2020.1839274.

Lazazzara, A., & Galanaki, E. (2018). "E-HRM adoption and usage: A cross-national analysis of enabling factors". In *Digital Technology and Organizational Change*, 125–140. Cham: Springer.

Li, X., Feng, H., Zhao, S., & Carter, D. A. (2021). The effect of revenue diversification on bank profitability and risk during the COVID-19 pandemic. *Finance Research Letters*, *43*, 101957.

Liboni, L., Cezarino, L., Jabbour, C., Oliveira, B., & Stefanelli, N. (2019). Smart industry and the pathways to HRM 4.0: Implications for SCM. *Supply Chain Management: An International Journal*, 24/1, 124–146. © Emerald Publishing Limited. ISSN 1359-8546, https://doi.org/10.1108/SCM-03-2018-0150.

Loesche, F., & Torre, I. (2020). *Creative Destruction, Encyclopedia of Creativity*, 3rd ed., (Vol. 1., pp. 226–231). https://doi.org/10.1016/B978-0-12-809324-5.23696-1.

Lorenz, M., Rübmann, M., Lasse, K., Lueth, K., & Bolle, M. (2015). *Man and Machine in Industry 4.0*. Boston: The Boston Consulting Group.

Loudon, D., & Della-Bitta, A. (1984). *Consumer Behaviour: Concepts and Applications*. 2nd ed. New York: McGraw-Hill.

Loxton, M., Truskett, R., Scarf, B., Sindone, L., Baldry, G., & Zhao, Y. (2020). Consumer behaviour during crises: Preliminary research on how coronavirus has manifested consumer panic buying, herd mentality, changing discretionary spending and the role of the media in influencing behaviour. *J. Risk Financial Manag.*, 13(8), 1–21. https://doi.org/10.3390/jrfm13080166.

Lu, H., Li, Y., Chen, M., Kim, H., & Serikawa, S. (2018). Brain intelligence: Go beyond artificial intelligence. *Mobile Networks and Applications*, 23(2), 368–375.

Lukes, S. (2013). *Emile Durkheim: The Division of Labour in Society*, 2nd ed. Hampshire: Palgrave Macmillan.

Mahiroğulları, A. (2005). Endüstri devrimi sonrasında emeğin istismarını belgeleyen İki Eser: germinal ve dokumacılar. *Sosyoloji Konferansları Dergisi*, 32, 41–53.

Makransky, G., Andreasen, N. K., Baceviciute, S., & Mayer, R. E. (2021). Immersive virtual reality increases liking but not learning with a science simulation and generative learning strategies promote learning in immersive virtual reality. *Journal of Educational Psychology, 113*(4), 719–735. https://doi.org/10.1037/edu0000473.

Man, F. (2017). *Çalışma hayatında eğitim ve geliştirme*. Sakarya: Sakarya Yayıncılık.

Mazzucato, M. (2020). *Giulio Quaggiotto the Big Failure of Small Government*. https://socialeurope.eu/the-big-failure-of-small-government.

Marshall, A. (1922). *Principles of Economics*. London, UK: Macmillan and Co.

Martens, L. (2009). "Gender and consumer behaviour". In *Contemporary Issues in Marketing and Consumer Behaviour*, 105–120. Oxford: Elsevier.

Marvel, M., Davis, J., & Sproul, C. (2016). Human capital and entrepreneurship research: A critical review and future directions. *November 2016 Entrepreneurship: Theory and Practice, 40*(3), 599–626 DOI:10.1111/etap.12136

Marx, K. (2015). Kapital, (Çev. Erkin Özalp, Mehmet Selik, Nail Satlıgan). İstanbul: Yordam Kitap.

Mathur, A., Moschis, G. P., & Lee, E. (2001). "A study of changes in brand preferences". In *AP – Asia Pacific Advances in Consumer Research Volume 4*, eds. Paula M. Tidwell & Thomas E. Muller. Provo, UT: Association for Consumer Research, pp. 133–139.

McGovern, S. L., Pandey, V., Gill, S., Aldrich, T., Myers, C., Desai, C., & Balasubramanian, V. (2018). *The New Age: Artificial Intelligence for Human Resource Opportunities and Functions*. London: Ernst & Young Press.

McKay, C., Ethan, P., & Alastair, F. (2019). *Automation and a Changing Economy – The Case for Action*. Washington D.C.: The Aspen Institute.

McKinsey & Company. (2017). The global forces inspiring a new narrative. *McKinsey Quarterly, 2017*(2), 32–52.

McKinsey'den Paydaş Kapitalizmi Raporu (2021). https://www.mckinsey.com/tr/our-insights/stakeholder-capitalism-report

McKinsey Global Institute. (2017). *Jobs Lost, Jobs Gained: Workforce Transitions in a Time of Automatio,* J. Manyika, S. Lund, M. Chui, J. Bughin, J. Woetzel, P. Batra, R. Ko, & Saurabh (). Sanghvi: McKinsey & Company

McNamara, K. R., & ve Newman, A. L. (2020). "The Big Reveal: Covid-19 and Globalization's Great Transformations", International Organization 74, Supplement, p. 1–19.

Meadows, D. H., Meadows D. L., Jorgen, R., & Behrens, W. W. (1972). *The Limits to Growth*. New York, US: Universe Books.

MEB (Milli Eğitim Bakanlığı). (2013). *Okul öncesi eğitim programı*. Ankara: Milli Eğitim Bakanlığı Yayınları.

Merlin, P. R., & Jayam, R. (2018). Artificial intelligence in human resource management. *International Journal of Pure and Applied Mathematics,* 119(14), 1891–1895.

Metin, Ş., & Aral, N. (2016). Proje yaklaşımına dayalı eğitimin beş yaş (60-72 ay) çocuklarının görsel algılarına etkisinin incelenmesi. *Eğitim ve Bilim,* 41(186), 149–162. Retrieved From: http://eb.ted.org.tr/index.php/EB/article/view/4594

Migliorelli, M., & Philippe, D. (Eds.). (2019). *Sustainability and Financial Risks the Impact of Climate Change, Environmental Degradation and Social Inequality on Financial Markets*. By Palgrave Studies in Impact Finance. Cham, Switzerland: Springer Nature.

Migliorelli, M. (2021). What do we mean by sustainable finance? Assessing existing frameworks and policy risks. *Sustainability* 13, 975.

Mihalcea, A. D. (2017). Employer branding and talent management in the digital age. *Management Dynamics in the Knowledge Economy,* 5(2), 289–306.

Milli Eğitim Bakanlığı. (2020b). Sanal sınıfların kullanımına ilişkin yazı. Retriewed From: http://fethiye.meb.gov.tr/meb_iys_dosyalar/2020_04/19120427_Sanal_SYnYf.pdf

Mor Çatı (2021). *Mor Çatı 2020 Yılı Faaliyet Raporu.* [Online] Available at: https://morcati.org.tr/faaliyet-raporlari/mor-cati-2020-yili-faaliyet-raporu/ [Accessed 01 09 2021].

Morrar, R., Arman, H., & Mousa, S. (2017). The fourth industrial revolution (industry 4.0): A social innovation perspective. *Technology Innovation Management Review, 7*(11), 12–20.

Muhdi, N., & Yuliejantiningsih, Y. (2020). The implementation of online learning in early childhood education during the Covid-19 Pandemic. *Jurnal Pendidikan Usia Dini,* 14(2), 247–261.

Mullins, L. (2010). *Management & Organizational Behaviour. 9e..* Essex: Pearson Education Ltd.

Murgai, A. (2018). Role of artificial intelligence in transforming human resource management. *International Journal of Trend İn Scientific Research and Development, 2*(3), 877–881.

Nabiyev, V. V. (2012). *Yapay zekâ insan bilgisayar etkileşimi.* Ankara: Seçkin Yayıncılık.

Nagaraj, A. (2021). *World Economic Forum.* [Online] Available at: https://www.weforum.org/agenda/2021/03/pandemic-shecession-womens-workplace-gains-gender-gap-covid/ [Accessed 20 05 2021].

Nerdrum, L., & Erikson, T. (2001). Intellectual capital: A human capital perspective. *Journal of Intellectual Capital, 2,* 127–135.

Newcomb, A. (2020). *Record number of women took over Fortune 500 companies in 2020.* [Online] Available at: https://www.nbcnews.com/business/business-news/record-number-women-took-over-fortune-500-companies-2020-n1252491 [Accessed 15 06 2021].

NielsenIQ. (2020, Mart 20). Key consumer behaviour thresholds identified as the coronavirus outbreak evolves. Aralık 4, 2020 NielsenIQ: https://nielseniq.com/global/en/insights/analysis/2020/key-consumerbehavior-thresholds-identified-as-the-coronavirus-outbreak-evolves-2

Nunes, M. L., Pereira, A. C., & Alves A. C. (2017). Smart products development approaches for Industry 4.0. *Procedia Manufacturing, 13,* 1215–1222.

OECD. (2021). *Employment: Time spent in paid and unpaid work, by sex.* [Online] Available at: https://stats.oecd.org/index.aspx?queryid=54757 [Accessed 25 06 2021].

OECD. (2021). *Gender wage gap.* [Online] Available at: https://data.oecd.org/earnwage/gender-wage-gap.htm [Accessed 28 06 2021].

OECD. (2020). *Building a Coherent Response for a Sustainable Post-COVID-19 Recovery, OECD Policy Responses to Coronavirus (COVID-19)*. Paris: OECD Publishing.

OECD. (2020); "Learning remotely when schools close: How well are students and schools prepared? Insights from PISA". https://www.oecd.org/coronavirus/policy-responses/learning-remotely-when-schools-close-how-well-are-students-and-schools-prepared-insights-from-pisa-3bfda1f7/

OECD. (2017a). *OECD Employment Outlook 2017*. Paris: OECD Publishing. https://doi.org/ 10.1787/empl_outlook-2017-en.

OECD. (2017b). *Investing in Climate, Investing in Growth*. Paris: OECD Publishing. https://doi.org/10.1787/9789264273528-en.

OECD. (2018[a]). *Policy Highlights Financing Climate Futures*. Paris: OECD Publishing.

OECD. 2018b., Nedelkoska, L., & Quintini, G. (2018). "Automation, skills use and training", OECD Social, Employment and Migration Working Papers, No. 202, OECD Publishing, Paris, https://doi.org/10.1787/2e2f4eea-en.

Onik, M., Miraz, M., & Kim, C. S. (2018). *A Recruitment and Human Resource Management Technique using Blockchain Technology for Industry 4.0*. IET Smart Cities Symposium 2018 (SCS'18). University of Bahrain, Bahrain, 1–6.

Orçan-Kaçan, M., & Kimzan, İ. (2017). Öğretmenlerin okul öncesi eğitimde teknoloji kullanımına ilişkin görüşlerinin incelenmesi. *INESJOURNAL Uluslararası Eğitim Bilimleri Dergisi. The Journal of International Education Science,* 4(12), 203–215. Retrieved From: https://dergipark.org.tr/en/download/article-file/563912

Özdoğan, O. (2018). *Endüstri 4.0: dördüncü sanayi devrimi ve endüstriyel dönüşümün anahtarları*. İstanbul: Pusula 20 Teknoloji ve A.Ş.

Özel, M. (1995). *Piyasa Düşmanı Kapitalizm*. İstanbul: İz Yayıncılık.

Özyürek, A. (2018). Okul öncesi çocukların bilgisayar teknolojileri kullanımının annelerin görüşlerine göre incelenmesi. *Çocuk ve Gelişim Dergisi/ Journal of Child and Development,* 2(2), 1–12. Retrieved From: https://dergipark.org.tr/en/pub/cg/issue/41609/467662

Padovano, F., & Emma, G. (2002). Comparing the Growth Effects of Marginal vs. Average Tax. Rates and progressivity. *European Journal of Political Economy, 18*(3), 529–544. DOI:10.1016/S0176-2680(02)00104-0

Pantano, E., Priporas, C.-V., Devereux, L., & Pizzi, G. (2021). Tweets to escape: Inter cultural differences in consumer expectations and risk behavior during the COVID-19 lockdown in three European countries. *Journal of Business Research*, 130, 59–69.

Papi, C., & ve Büyükaslan, A. (2007). *Developments in Distance Education in Turkey and France: Which Educational Right*. Marseille: Colloque Tice Mediterranee – Human / Exchange in Distance Education.

Pellegrini, C., Rizzi, F., & Frey, M. (2018). The role of sustainable human resource practices in influencing employee behaviour for corporate sustainability. *Business Strategy and The Environment*, 28(8), 1221–1232.

Pereira, A. C., & ve Romero, F. (2017). A review of the meanings and the implications of the Industry 4.0 concept. *Procedia Manufacturing*, 13, 1206–1214.

Peters M. A., & Jandric P. (2015). Philosophy of education in the age of digital reason (PDF). *Review of Contemporary Philosophy*, 14, 162–181. ISSN 1841–5261.

Pigou, A. C. (1920). *The Economics of Welfare*, 1st ed. London: Macmillan and Co.

Piketty, T., Emmanuel, S., & Stefanie, S. (2014). Optimal taxation of top labor incomes: A tale of three elasticities. *American Economic Journal: Economic Policy*, 6, 230–271.

Piketty, T. (2013). *Capital in the 21st Century*. Cambridge, MA: Harvard Univ. Press.

Powell, G. (2011). The gender and leadership wars. *Organizational Dynamics*, 40(1), 1–9.

Puttaiah, M. H., Raverkar, A. K., & Avramakis, E. (2020). Allchange: How COVID-19 is transforming consumer behaviour, Swiss Re Institute,Published on:10 Dec 2020, https://www.swissre.com/institute/research/topics-and-risk-dialogues/health-and-longevity/covid-19-and-consumer-behaviour.html,10/10/2021.

PWC. (2020). The consumer transformed, Global Consumer Insights Survey 2020.

PWC. (2020). *Implications of COVID-19 Crisis for the Turkish Banking Sector*. PWC Press. https://www.pwc.com.tr/covid-19-banking-sector

Robin, B. R. (2008). Digital storytelling: A powerful technology tool for the 21st century classroom. *Theory into Practice*, 47(3), 220–228. Retrieved From: https://digitalstorytellingclass.pbworks.com/f/ +Storytelling+A+Powerful.pdf

Rowley, K., Bunker, E., & ve Cole, D. (2002). Designing the right blend: Combining online and onsite training for optimal results. *Performance Improvement*, 41(4), 24–34.

Russel, S., & Norwig, P. (2010). *Artificial Intelligence: A Modern Approach*. New Jersey: Prentice Hall.

Sadik, A. (2008). Digital Digital storytelling: A meaningful technology-integrated approach for engaged student learning. *Educational Technology Research and Development*, 56(4), 487–506. Retrieved From: https://www.researchgate.net/publication/225696853_Digital_storytelling_A_meaningful_technology-integrated_approach_for_engaged_student_learning

Sak, R., Şahin Sak, İ., & Nas, E. (2020). Pandemi sürecinde okul öncesi eğitim. F. Tahnan ve H.İ. Özok (Ed). Pandemi ve eğitim. (s.161–189). Ankara: Anı Yayıncılık.

Sangster, A., Stoner, G., & Flood, B. (2020). Insights into accounting education in a COVID-19 world. *Accounting Education*, 29(5), 431–562. Retrieved From: https://doi.org/10.1080/09639284.2020.1808487

Sapsağlam, Ö. (2018). Social media awareness and usage in preschool children. International *Journal of Eurasia Social Sciences,* 9(31), 728–746. Retrieved From: https://app.trdizin.gov.tr/makale/TXpFeE16WXhNUT09/social-media-awareness-and-usage-in-preschool-children

Sarıtaş, E., & Barutçu, S.(2020). Öğretimde dijital dönüşüm ve öğrencilerin çevrimiçi öğrenmeye hazır bulunuşluluğu: pandemi dönemi. *İnternet Uygulamaları ve Yönetimi Dergisi,* 11(1), 5–22. Retrieved From: https://dergipark.org.tr/en/pub/iuyd/issue/54593/706397

Schoenmaker, D. (2017). *From Risk to Opportunity: A Framework for Sustainable Finance.* Rotterdam, The Netherlands: Rotterdam School of Management, Erasmus University.

Schuler, R. S., & Jackson, S. E. (1987). Linking competitive strategies with human resource management practices. *The Academy of Management,* 1(3), 207–219.

Schumpeter, J. A. (2007). *Kapitalizm, sosyalizm ve demokrasi,* 2nd ed. Ankara: Alter.

Schwab, K. (2017). *Dördüncü Sanayi Devrimi.* İstanbul: Optimist Yayınevi.

Schwab, K. (2019). *Dördüncü sanayi devrimini şekillendirmek.* İstanbul: Optimist Yayınları.

Schwab, K. (2020a). A Better Economy Is Possible. But We Need to Reimagine Capitalism to Do It. Retrieved from Time: https://time.com/collection/ great-reset/5900748/klaus-schwab-capitalism/

Schwab, K., & Kroos, H. (1971). *Modern Company Management in Mechanical Engineering.* Frankfurt/Main-Niederrad: Verein Deutscher MaschinenbauAnstalten.

Schwab, K., & Thierry, M. (2020). *Covid-19: The Great Reset.* Forum Publishing.

Selçuk, Z. (2020). Presentation of the Budget For, Ministry of National Education, https://sgb.meb.gov.tr/meb_iys_dosyalar/2019_12/18094404_2020_BUTCE_SUNUYU_17.12.2019.pdf

Sezgin, S. (2021). Acil uzaktan eğitim sürecinin analizi: Öne çıkan kavramlar, sorunlar ve çıkarılan dersler. *Anadolu Üniversitesi Sosyal Bilimler Dergisi,* 21(1), 273–296. Retrieved From: https://dergipark.org.tr/en/pub/ausbd/issue/60870/902616

Shamim, S., Cang, S., Yu, H., & Li, Y. (2016). *Management Approaches for Industry 4.0: A Human Resources Management Perspective.* 2016 IEEE Congress on Evolutionary Computation, 5309–5316.

Sheth, J. (2020). Impact of Covid-19 on consumerbehavior: Willtheoldhabitsreturnordie? *Journal of Business Research,* 117, 280–283.

Sirer, E. (2020). Eğitimin ekran üzerinden teknolojik dönüşümünde pandemi dönemi'nin etkisi. OPUS–*Uluslararası Toplum Araştırmaları Dergisi,* 16(29), 1987–2018. doi: 10.26466/opus.777215. Retrieved Form: https://dergipark.org.tr/en/pub/opus/article/777215

Skalická, V., Belsky, J., Stenseng, F., & Wichstrøm, L. (2015). Preschool-age problem behavior and teacher–child conflict in school: Direct and moderation effects by preschool organization. *Child Development,* 86(3), 955–964. Retrieved From: https://srcd.onlinelibrary.wiley.com/doi/abs/10.1111/cdev.12350

Solekhah, H. (2020). Distance Learning of Indonesian Early Childhood Education (PAUD) during the Covid-19 Pandemic. *International Journal of Emerging Issues in Early Childhood Education(IJEIECE),* 2(2),105–119. Retrieved From: https://www.researchgate.net/publication/347278027_Distance_Learning_of_Indonesian_Early_Childhood_Education_PAUD_during_the_Covid-19_Pandemic

Solow, R. M. (1986). On the intergenerational allocation of natural resources. *The Scandinavian Journal of Economics,* 88(1), Growth and Distribution: Intergenerational Problems (Mar., 1986), 141–149.

Sosyal ve Ekonomi Araştırmaları Dergisi (ASEAD), 7(5), 251–268.

Stats, N. Z. (2021). *Population.* [Online] Available at: https://www.stats.govt.nz/topics/population [Accessed 01 09 2021].

Staub, S., Karaman, E., Kaya, S., Karapınar, H., & Güven, E. (2015). Artificial neural network and agility. *Procedia – Social and Behavioral Sciences,* 195, 1477–1485. DOI:10.1016/j.sbspro.2015.06.448.

Steffen, W., Katherine, R., Johan, R., Cornell S. E., Ingo, F., Bennett Elena M., Reinette, B., Carpenter Stephen R., de Vries Wim, de Wit Cynthia A., Carl, F., Dieter, G., Jens, H., Mace Georgina, M., Persson Linn, M., Veerabhadran, R., Belinda, R., & Sverker, S. (2015). Planetary boundaries: Guiding human development on a changing planet. *Science,* 347(6223), 736–47.

Stiglitz, J. E. (1989). Markets, market failures, and development. *American Economic Review*, 79(2), 197–203.

Stiglitz, J. E. (2016). Inequality and economic growth. *The Political Quarterly*, 86(S1), 134–155.

Strohmeier, S., & Piazza, F. (2015). Artificial intelligence techniques in human resource management—A conceptual exploration. In C. Kahraman, & S. Onar (Eds.), *Intelligent Techniques in Engineering Management*, 149–172. Cham: Springer International Publishing.

Süleymanlı, E. (2020, Ağustos 10). Pandemi Sonrası Süreçte Alışkanlıklarımız Değişecek. e-koronafobi: https://npistanbul.com/koronavirus/pandemi-sonrasi-surecte-aliskanliklarimiz-degisecek

Şahin, B. (2006). Okul öncesi dönemde bilgisayar destekli fen öğretimi ve etkilerinin incelenmesi. Yüksek Lisans Tezi, İstanbul: Yeditepe Üniversitesi Sosyal Bilimler Enstitüsü.

Şeker, S. E. (2014). "Maslow'un İhtiyaçlar Piramiti", YBS Ansiklopedi, Cilt.1,Sayı.1,S.43–45.

Şener, G., & Gündüzalp, S., (2018). Akademisyenlerin Üniversitelerde Dijital Dönüşüm ile İlgili Görüşleri., 1. Uluslararası Battal Gazi Mutidisipliner çalışmalar kongresi Tam Metin Kitabı Cilt 1, 177–182.

Tabor, S. W. (2007). Narrowing the Distance: Implementing a Hybrid Learning Model for Information Security Education. *Quarterly Review of Distance Education*, 8(1), 47–57. Retrieved January 14, 2019, from https://www.learntechlib.org/p/106717/.

Tambe, P., Cappelli, P., & Yakubovich, V. (2019). Artificial intelligence in human resources management: Challenges and a path forward. *California Management Review*, 61(4), 15–42.

The World Bank. (2021). *Population, Total - Iceland.* [Online]Available at: https://data.worldbank.org/indicator/SP.POP.TOTL?locations=IS [Accessed 01 09 2021].

The World Bank. (2021). *Population, Total - Sweden.* [Online] Available at: https://data.worldbank.org/indicator/SP.POP.TOTL?locations=SE [Accessed 01 09 2021].

Toran, M. (2021). Yeni Normalde Erken Çocukluk Eğitimi ve Bakımı: Eleştirel Bir Değerlendirme *Eleştirel Pedagoji*, 68. Retrieved From: http://www.elestirelpedagoji.com/FileUpload/ks7397/File/68_mehmet_toran.pdf

Toran, M., Sak, R., Xu, Y., Şahin-Sak, İ. T., & Yu, Y. (2021). Parents and children during the COVID-19 quarantine process: Experiences from Turkey and China. *Journal of Early Childhood Research*, 1–19. Retrieved From: https://doi.org/10.1177/1476718X20977583

Treven, S. (2000). The importance of human resource management for the success of the company. *Management*, 5(1), 83–93.

Tuğluk, M. N., & Özkan, B. (2019) MEB 2013 Okul Öncesi Eğitim Programının 21. yüzyıl becerileri açısından analizi. *Temel Eğitim Dergisi,* 1(4), 29–38. Retrieved From: https://dergipark.org.tr/en/download/article-file/875766

TUIK. (2021). *Labour Force by Household Population.* [Online] Available at: https://data.tuik.gov.tr/Kategori/GetKategori?p=Nufus-ve-Demografi-109[Accessed 25 06 2021].

Tunç, A., & Atıcı, F. Z. (2020). Dünyada ve Türkiye'de pandemilerle mücadele: risk ve kriz yönetimi bağlamında bir değerlendirme. *Troyacademy*, 5(2), 329–362, doi: 10.314454/usb.808685. Retrieved From: https://dergipark.org.tr/en/pub/usb/article/808685

Turan, Türkan (2008), *İktisadi Büyüme Teorisine Giriş*. İstanbul: Yalın yayıncılık.

Türkel,S.,&Yeşilkuş,F.(2020).DİJİTALDÖNÜŞÜMPARADİGMASI:ENDÜSTRİ 4.0 . Avrasya Sosyal ve Ekonomi Araştırmaları Dergisi, COVID-19 ÖZEL SAYISI 2, 332–346. Retrieved from https://dergipark.org.tr/tr/pub/asead/issue/54658/726985

Turkish Statistical Institute; Household Information Technologies (IT) Usage Survey. (2020). https://data.tuik.gov.tr/Bulten/Index?p=Hanehalki-Bilisim-Teknolojileri-(BT)-Kullanim-Arastirmasi-2020-33679

Tutkun, Ö. F., & Aksoyalp, Y. (2010). 21. Yüzyılda Öğretmen Yetiştirme Eğitim Programının Boyutları . *Selçuk Üniversitesi Sosyal Bilimler Enstitüsü Dergisi, 24*, 361–371. Retrieved From https://dergipark.org.tr/en/pub/susbed/issue/61801/924630

Ulagay, O. (2021). Korona'dan paydaşlar kapitalizmine. Retrieved from Dünya Gazetesi: https://www.dunya.com/kose-yazisi/koronadan-paydaslarkapitalizmine/608576

Uluser-İnan, N. (2003). Okul öncesinde bilgisayar kullanımı. In M. Sevinç (Ed.), Erken Çocuklukta Gelişim ve Eğitimde Yeni Yaklaşımlar (s. 212-219) içinde. İstanbul: Morpa.

Umbrelle, S. (2021). *Should We Reset? A Review of Klaus Schwab and Thierry Malleret's 'COVID 19: The Great Reset.* Retrieved from Journal of Value Inquiry: https://link.springer.com/article/10.1007/s10790-021-09794- 1#citeas

UN Women. (2020a). COVID-19 and its economic toll on women: The story behind the numbers. [Online] Available at: https://www.unwomen.org/en/news/stories/2020/9/feature-covid-19-economic-impacts-on-women?gclid=EAIaIQobChMI-pu38vGK8QIVAWEYCh0k6A79EAAYASAAEgKr-PD_BwE [Accessed 25 06 2021].

UN Women (2020b.) *From Insights to Action: Gender Equality in the Wake of Covid-19.* [Online] Available at: https://www.unwomen.org/en/digital-library/publications/2020/09/gender-equality-in-the-wake-of-covid-19 [Accessed 29 06 2021].

UNCTAD. (2021). *COVID-19 threatens four 'lost decades' for gender equality.* [Online] Available at: https://unctad.org/news/covid-19-threatens-four-lost-decades-gender-equality [Accessed 01 10 2021].

UNCTAD, World Investment Report. (2020). Issued by the United Nations Conference on Trade and Development, New York 2020, United Nations Publications.

UNESCO. (2021). *Covid-19 Impact of Education Data Paris: UNESCO.* Retrieved From:

UNESCO. (2020a). *COVID-19 Educational Disruption and Response.* Retrieved April 29, 2020, from https://en.unesco.org/covid19/educationresponse

United Nations Development Programme. (2020a). *The Economic Impacts of COVID-19 and Gender Inequality Recommendations for Policymakers.* United Nations.

United Nations Environment Programme – Finance Initiative (UNEP-FI). (2017). *Principles for Positive Impact Finance.* Accessible at: https://www.unepfi.org/positive-impact/principles-for-positive-impact-finance/

United Nations Environment Programme – Finance Initiative (UNEP-FI). (2018). *Rethinking Impact to Finance SDGs.* Accessible at: https://www.unepfi.org/positive-impact/rethinking-impact/

United Nations Environment Programme – Finance Initiative (UNEP-FI). (2019). *Principles for Responsible Banking.* Accessible at https://www.unepfi.org/banking/bankingprinciples/ resources-for-implementation/

United Nations. (2021a). *World Economic Situation and Prospects 2021.* New York: United Nations.

United Nations (2021b). *World Economic Situation and Prospects as of Mid-2021.* New York: United Nations.

United Nations. (2020). *The Sustainable Development Goals Report 2020.* New York: United Nations Publications.

Uşun, Salih (2006). *Distance Education.* Ankara: Nobel Publication Distribution.

Vargas-Lopez, A., Cicatiello, C., Principato, L., & Secondi, L. (2021). Consumer expenditure, elasticity and value of food waste: A Quadratic Almost Ideal Demand System fore valuating changes in Mexicoduring COVID-19, Socio-Economic Planning Sciences, In Press, Corrected Proof, https://doi.org/10.1016/j.seps.2021.101065, pp.1–10.

Vatandaş, S. (2020). "McKinsey Araştırması: COVID-19 Kriziyle Değişen Tüketici Harcamaları ve Türkiye", https://www.sivilsayfalar.org/2020/05/04/mckinsey-arastirmasi-covid-19-kriziyle-degisen-tuketici-harcamalari-ve-turkiye/, Erişim: 21/07/2020.

Vosloo Willem Benjamin. (2014). The Theories of Thomas Piketty, Karl Marx and Simon Kuznets on Wealth Inequality. Not published, Wollongong, July 2014. Available at: https://irp-cdn.multiscreensite.com/6a3663e1/files/ uploaded/

Wamba, S. F., Akter, S., Edwards, A., Chopin, G., & Gnanzou, D. (2015). How big data can make big impact-findings from a systematic review and a longitudinal case study. *International Journal of Production Economics*, 165(1), 234–246.

Wang, G., Zhang, Y. I., Zhao, J., Zhang, J., & Jiang, F. (2020). Mitigate the effects of home confinement on children during the Covid-19 outbreak. *The Lancet*, doi:10.1016/s0140-6736(20)30547-x. Retrieved From: https://www.thelancet.com/journals/lancet/article/PIIS0140-6736(20)30547-X/fulltext

Wang, T. (2019). Thoughts on salary reform in the digital age. *Advances in Economics, Business and Management Research*, 96(4), 198–201.

Warrell, M. (2021). Women are quitting: How we can curb the 'She-Cession' and support working women. [Online] Available at: https://www.forbes.com/sites/margiewarrell/2021/01/06/does-a-she-cession-loom-how-to-better-support-women-through-this-pandemic/?sh=78d7f98d3ece [Accessed 25 06 2021].

We are Social (2020). Dijital in 2020. Retrieved From: https://wearesocial.com/digital-2020.

Weber, M. (1999). Protestan Ahlakı ve Kapitalizmin Ruhu (Çev. Zeynep Gürata). İstanbul: Ayraç Yayınları.

Wharton, A. S. (2012). *The Sociology of Gender: An Introduction to Theory and Research*, 2nd ed. Oxford: Wiley-Blackwell.

Williamson, J., & Mahar, M. (2002). *"Finansal Liberalizasyon Üzerine Bir İnceleme", (Çev) Güven Delice*. Ankara: Liberte Yayınları.

Wójcik, D., & Ioannou, S. (2020). COVID-19 and finance: Market developments so far and potential impacts on the financial sector and centres. *Tijdschrift voor economische en sociale geografie*, 111(3), 387–400.

Wolgemuth, J., Savage, R., Helmer, J., Bottrell, C., Lea, T., Harper, H., Halkitis, K., & Abrami, P. (2011). Using computer-based instruction to improve indigenous early literacy in Northern Australia: A quasi-experimental study. *Australasian Journal of Educational Technology*, 27(4), 727–750. Retrieved From: http://www.ascilite.org.au/ajet/ajet27/wolgemuth.html

World Economic Forum Strategic Intelligence (2020). https://intelligence.weforum.org/

World Health Organization (WHO). (2020). WHO director-genaral's opening remarks at the media briefing on Covid-19. Retrieved From: https://who.int/dg/speeches/detail

World Inequality Lab. (2017). "World Inequality Report 2018." by Facundo Alvaredo, Lucas Chancel, Thomas Piketty, Emmanuel Saez, and Gabriel Zucman (coordinators). Paris: World Inequality Lab.

World Social Report. (2020). *Issued by United Nations Department of Economic and Social Affairs*. New York 2020: United Nations Publications.

Xie, Z., & Yang, J. (2020). Autonomous learning of elementary students at home during the COVID-19 epidemic: A case study of the Second Elementary School in Daxie, Ningbo, Zhejiang Province, China. *Best Evidence of Chinese Education*, 4(2), 535–541.

Yalçın, V., Simsar, A., & Dinler, H. (2020). 5-6 Yaş Cocukları için 21. Yy Becerileri Ölçeği (DAY-2): Geçerlik ve Güvenirlik Çalışması. *Akdeniz Eğitim Araştırmaları Dergisi,* 14(32), 78–97. doi: 10.29329/mjer.2020.258.5. Retrieved From: https://toad.halileksi.net/sites/default/files/pdf/5-6-yas-cocuklari-icin-21-yy-becerileri-olcegi-day-2-toad.pdf

YaleNews. (2012). Scientists not immune from gender bias, Yale study shows. [Online] Available at: https://news.yale.edu/2012/09/24/scientists-not-immune-gender-bias-yale-study-shows [Accessed 01 09 2021].

Yamamoto, G. T., & Altun, D. (2020). Coronavirüs ve Çevrimiçi (Online) Eğitimin Önlenemeyen Yükselişi. Üniversite Araştırmaları Dergisi, 3(1), 25–34. https://doi.org/10.26701/uad.711110

Yawalkar, V. V. (2019). Study of artificial intelligence and its role in human resource management. *International Journal of Research and Analytical Reviews (IJRAR)*, 6(1) 20–24.

Yıldız, A. (2020). Kriz dönemlerinde tüketici davranışlarının incelenmesi. *Uluslararası Sosyal Bilimler Akademi Dergisi*, 2(3), 377–390.

Yılmazsoy, B., Özdinç, F., & Kahraman, M. (2018). Sanal sınıf ortamındaki sınıf yönetimine yönelik öğrenci görüşlerinin incelenmesi. *Trakya Eğitim Dergisi,* 8(3), 513–525. Retrieved From: https://dergipark.org.tr/tr/download/article-file/481703

YÖK. (2020). Yükseköğretim Kurulu. Retrieved from https://www.yok.gov.tr/Sayfalar/Haberler/2020/universitelerde-uygulanacak-uzaktan-egitime-ilis kin-aciklama.aspx

Yuen, K. F., Leong, J. Z. Er.,Wong, Wang, Y., & Xueqin, D. (2021). Panic buying during COVID-19: Survival psychology and needs perspectives in deprived environments. *International Journal of Disaster Risk Reduction*, 62, 1–12.

Zaoui, F., & Souissi, N. (2020). Roadmap for digital transformation: A literature review. *Procedia Computer Science*, 175, 621–628. http://dx.doi.org/10.1016/i.procs.2020.07.09Q

Zarrilli, S., & Luomaranta, H. (2021). Gender and unemployment: Lessons from the COVID-19 pandemic. [Online] Available at: https://unctad.org/news/gender-and-unemployment-lessons-covid-19-pandemic [Accessed 25 06 2021].

Zheng, X., Ruan, C., & Zheng, L. (2021). Money orlove? The impact of the COVID-19 pandemic on consumer life goals and subjective well-being. *Journal of Business Research*, 137, 626–633.

Zhong, R. Y., Huang, G. Q., Dai, Q. Y., & Zhang, T. (2017). Intelligent manufacturing in the context of industry 4.0 a review. *Engineering*, 3(5), 616–630.

Zhou, L., Li, F., Shanshan, W., & Zhou, M. (2020). 'School's Out, But Class' On', the largest online education in the world today: Taking China's practical exploration during the COVID-19 epidemic prevention and control as an example. *SSRN Electronic Journal*, 4(2). https://doi.org/10.2139 /ssrn.3555520

Zidar, O. (2015). "Tax Cuts for Whom? Heterogeneous Effects of Tax Changes on Growth and Employment" University of Chicago Working Paper, March 2015. Published Version: in *Journal of Political Economy*, 127(3), 1437–1472. June 2019.

Ziolo, M., Zofia, F. B., Iwona, B., Katarzyna, C., Mihaela, T. D., & Isabel, N.-C. (2019). Finance, sustainability and negative externalities: An overview of the European context. *Sustainability*, 11, 4249.

www.ingramcontent.com/pod-product-compliance
Ingram Content Group UK Ltd.
Pitfield, Milton Keynes, MK11 3LW, UK
UKHW041143300926
15471UKWH00012B/126

9 783631 867952